Guiding Light

Trust and Transform
CYCLE C

Homilies by Fr. Joe Robinson

Shepherds of Christ Publications
P.O. Box 627
China, Indiana 47250 USA

Toll free USA: (888) 211-3041
Tel: (812) 273-8405
Fax: (812) 273-3182
Email: info@sofc.org
http://www.sofc.org

ISBN: 978-1-934222-48-5

Second Printing: 2016

Dedicated to Pope Francis

In Honor of Our Beloved Priests

98th Anniversary of Fatima
October 13, 2015

My dear priests, hierarchy and members of the mystical body of Christ,

I give my heart to Jesus and Mary with you in love.

Fr. Carter our founder wrote two very important books *Response to God's Love* and *Response in Christ*.

The following thoughts are inspired by these two books.

God first loved us.

We receive a sharing in Divine Life in baptism – our knowing and loving capacity is elevated.

We are human creatures and yet we see God's loving self-communication to us with our concomitant response to Him in love.

Man rejected this self-communication of God in original sin.

God on His part communicates His own life through grace and man in return gives himself to God and his fellowman in loving service.

We can respond to this marvelous gift God gives to us as members of the mystical body of Christ – with Christ our head.

We can be witnesses of Christ alive in us both in the Church and in the world because the Father, Son and Holy Spirit dwell in a special way, in our graced, baptized soul.

God wants such intimacy with us.

I, Rita Robinson Ring, have learned a lot about the spiritual life from Our Lord in daily Mass and in spending at least one hour a day before the Blessed Sacrament where Jesus is truly present in His Divinity and humanity, no less present than when He walked the earth.

I have been guided by Fr. Carter our founder and had the gift of my brother, Fr. Joe Robinson at Mass, Sunday, week days, funerals etc. and other priests who have helped us on our journey in Shepherds of Christ.

Through the Priestly Newsletter of Fr. Carter we circulated 17,000,000 Newsletters to Priests and Hierarchy since 1994. This is Fr. Joe's 9th book. We sent out most years to about 38,000 priests and hierarchy. We have circulated about 300,000 of Fr. Joe's homily books over 8 years to priests and hierarchy.

What a gift these homilies of Fr. Joe's are as he teaches us about Responding to God's love, being Christ a-live in this world as a witness to Jesus and teaching us about the Bread of Life: the Word and the Eucharist.

We pray for the priests and have since 1994 in prayer chapters. Our prayers have been translated in 8 languages with the *Imprimatur*. We especially pray 8 days every month with Mass and the Holy Eucharist exposed most of the days for the priests, the Church and the world. We pray 24 hours every day and night in China before the exposed Eucharist for the priests and the Church.

Please pray with us, the prayers, Fr. Carter, our Founder, gave us in 1994 centered in Consecration to the Hearts of Jesus and Mary praying for the priests, the Church and the world. Life is in Jesus.

With love,

Rita Robinson Ring and all at Shepherds of Christ

We want Adoration Chapels
around the world –
The Mighty Medicine

Table of Contents
Cycle C – 2015 / 2016

Certificate of Marriage

I, the undersigned, do hereby certify, that on the 25 day of June A.D. 19 36
in the church of St. Boniface I joined in the

Holy Bonds of Matrimony

William M. Robinson and Alice Weber

according to the rites of the Holy Roman Catholic Church.

Witness: Henry J. Robinson
Marie Weber

Rev. John H. Schwartz
Pastor

Dedicated to William and Alice Robinson.

Our Mother and Father married on
June 25, 1936 in St. Boniface Church, Cincinnati.

1st Sunday of Advent
December 2, 2012

INTRODUCTION – (Jeremiah 33:14-16; 1 Thess. 3: 12-4:2; Luke 21:25-28, 34-36) The prophet, Jeremiah, lived during the most devastating time in the history of Israel. He witnessed the Babylonian invasion which brought with it the destruction of Jerusalem and its sacred Temple that had been built by King Solomon. He saw many of his fellow citizens enslaved and taken into exile. Yet his words reflect hope and not despair. His hope is based not on human capabilities but on God's faithfulness to God's promises made to God's people, promises made over 400 years earlier - during the reign of King David. God would bring to the throne a family member of the House of David, a just shoot, who would bring peace and security to Jerusalem. We still wait for peace and security - not only in Jerusalem but all over the world. The promised one from David's line has begun his reign. The gospel tells us one day he will come in great glory to complete his work and to establish the kingdom of God forever.

HOMILY – I want to start by briefly describing 1000 years of Jewish history for you. 1000 years before Christ, David was king. His son Solomon succeeded him and built a Temple in Jerusalem. He built a lot of other stuff too, including temples for the gods his many pagan wives worshipped. His building programs bankrupted the country and when he died, the northern part of the country revolted against the new king, King David's grandson, and they chose their own king. The northern kingdom suffered many uprisings and changes of leadership and eventually in 722 B.C. they were completely annihilated by the Assyrians (warriors from northern Iraq). Meanwhile, the southern portion of the

Holy Land, now known as Judah, continued to be ruled by David's descendants, but the kingdom began to unravel about 600 B.C. In 587 B.C. the Babylonians came down on Jerusalem, destroyed everything and showed no mercy. Most of the Jews were taken as slaves to Babylon. That's what I spoke about in my introduction. From then on, for the next 600 years, Judah had no king of its own. It suffered under the control of foreign nations: first the Babylonians, then the Persians, followed by the Greeks, then the Syrians and, finally, the Romans. This brings us up to the time of Jesus. Being under the Romans was difficult. The people lived in poverty because of taxes and had little say as to how they were governed. Different groups of Jews dealt with their oppression in different ways. I'm going to mention four ways by which people tended to respond. 1)There were those who silently suffered under Roman occupation. They knew, humanly speaking, they could not stand up to the Romans. 2) Some Jews took more daring actions and attempted nonviolent protests. For the most part, Rome came back strong against the protesters; however, they occasionally backed down because of the protests. 3) Then there were Jews who believed that God had given the Jews the land of Israel and that it should be taken back by force from the Roman rulers. Zealots would have been among this group. Zealots were like modern day terrorists. They would even kill their fellow Jews who would not join in their rebellion. The Zealot movement led to various revolts against Rome (too many to mention) during which thousands of Jews were slaughtered. The Romans tolerated no opposition.

A fourth form of protest is the one in which we are especially interested. It developed as a sort of "religious" protest. It was an idea or an ideology called "apocalypticism" which I have been talking about the past two Sundays. The Essenes, who composed the Dead Sea Scrolls, were of this thinking. The apocalyptic approach was based on the viewpoint that our world was controlled by evil powers; even with all our ingenuity and cleverness, we could do nothing about it. One must wait for God to act to free our world from the evil powers that dominate. Once God does this, only God can establish a world ruled by the forces of goodness and righteousness (aka the kingdom of God). Apocalyptic thinkers were especially interested in when this was going to happen. The Apostles were especially interested in when this would come about because they believed (as we do) that Jesus was the Messiah who would initiate the Kingdom of God, and they expected to have an important place in that Kingdom. The apocalyptic view was that this would happen in a very short time and people must be ready, living a good life, to be part of God's kingdom. Those who were not prepared to enter into God's kingdom would suffer eternal sorrow.

This apocalyptic way of thinking is behind today's gospel. The gospel tells us the evil world as we know it is to come to an end. It will be replaced by God's world where holiness, goodness, peace and love will prevail. Three things stand out in today's readings:

1) This kingdom where holiness and justice will prevail will come into existence through one of King David's descendants: "I will raise up for David a just shoot". The next three weeks will be focused on celebrating the birth of the One God has raised up. How will we prepare? Will prayer be a part of our preparations? A lot of people don't pray because they find it too hard. The hardest thing about prayer is to take time for it.

2) We can lament all the bad things that happen in today's world, but we cannot let them destroy us. Christians need to be optimistic. Jesus tells us when we see the signs that the Son of Man is coming (and we can see these signs more clearly through prayer and Scripture reading), we should not go around depressed. We should stand erect and raise our heads because our redemption is at hand.

3) And third, Jesus tells us to be careful our hearts do not become drowsy (the Greek word also means being weighed down, burdened) with three things: carousing or drunkenness (I know this doesn't apply to anyone here - but what about the third thing, "the anxieties of daily life." Isn't this good advice at this time of year when we can get so weary and burdened down with the "stuff" that keeps us from focusing on what Christ's coming is all about?

Our readings give us the push we all need as we start the season of Advent, so that when December 26 comes we don't just collapse and say, "thank God it's over."

2nd Sunday of Advent
December 9, 2012

INTRODUCTION – (Baruch 5:1-9; Philippians 1:4-6, 8-11; Luke 3:1-6) In today's first reading, we hear from Baruch, the secretary of Jeremiah the prophet. He lived during the Babylonian exile over 500 years before Christ. Our first reading has the Babylonian invasion and destruction of Jerusalem as its background. Baruch speaks to the devastated city of Jerusalem and tells it to rejoice for it will prosper again. With the vision of a prophet, he tells Jerusalem to look east (toward Babylon) and see God gathering his people together to bring them back home. It is indeed a message of hope. This return of the exiles to Jerusalem is also poetically described in the Book of the prophet Isaiah. John the Baptist, who was sent to prepare the way for the Messiah, borrows from Isaiah to describe his own mission.

HOMILY – Christ came down to us to lead us to God. He came from on high, the Son of God, co-eternal with the Father and the Holy Spirit, and took on our human flesh. St. John says it so simply: "in the beginning was the Word, and the Word was with God and the Word was God." "And the Word became flesh and made his dwelling among us, and we saw his glory, the glory as of the Father's only Son, full of grace and truth." This mystery of God becoming human is expressed theologically in the term: Incarnation. We say it every Sunday: "by the Holy Spirit, (he - Jesus) was incarnate of the Virgin Mary, and became man."

We are preparing to celebrate his birth among us. We tend to celebrate many births, but Jesus' birth is indeed worth celebrating. It was an event that had no equal. It was not only marvelous because it was God coming among us, sharing in our own human flesh, but as I said when I started, he came down to us in order to lead us to God. Bringing us to God is the main theme of today's readings. The liturgy uses the return of the Jewish exiles from Babylon to their home in Jerusalem as a symbol of our coming to God. Baruch explains it so beautifully in today's first reading: "God is leading Israel in joy by the light of his glory." John the Baptist quotes Isaiah when he describes his mission to prepare for the coming of our Savior. He said he was "a voice crying out in the desert: prepare the way of the Lord, make straight his paths." John was calling people to holiness so that God himself could lead them.

It is to holiness that our liturgy is calling us today. As we celebrate Christ's birth, is our celebration going to bring us a little closer to God, or is it just a ritual of decorating and undecorating, trading gifts, having parties and just wearing ourselves out. Coming closer to God, knowing his presence and his love for us is what it is all about. John the Baptist is speaking to us today: "make straight his paths." Get obstacles out of his way so he can fill our lives with his presence.

This is an ongoing effort for we are always called to grow in our relationship with God.

There are many ways we can prepare spiritually. I am going to offer two things that might help. One is the little booklet at the doors of the church called the *Word Among Us*. It has the scripture readings for every day of Advent and gives a brief reflection on them. It probably wouldn't take more than five or ten minutes to read and reflect on. As I said last week, the hardest thing about prayer is sitting down to do it.

The other thing I wish to offer is my homily book. It follows the Sunday readings for this year. It has most of the homilies I preached three years ago when we were reading from Luke's gospel (cycle C). They are not the same homilies I am preaching this year even though the readings are the same. So the homily book will give you another perspective on the Scriptures for each Sunday.

There is one more thing I want to mention, which has nothing to do with anything I've said so far, but I need to say it. We are going to discontinue burning candles at the side altars. We now have two electric vigil light stands. Personally I never cared for the electric type, but many churches now use them. They are easier and less expensive to maintain, and most of all they do not smoke up the walls and the ceiling. We just spent a lot of money to make our church clean and beautiful and it doesn't make much sense to smoke it up again. Sometimes in lighting the candles, the taper or stick fell into the candle and it started a fire. It never caused a major problem, it was just a smelly one when the plastic started to burn. To light a candle simply press a button. It will burn for five days. The offering is still the same: $2.00. Making an offering and saying a little prayer is part of the ritual of burning a candle in Church. It is the same as before as long as the sacrifice of an offering, a little prayer and the intention is there. And it will help keep our church clean. Right now we have only two vigil light stands. If we need to get one or two more we will, depending on their use. I just wanted to explain what we did and why we did it.

And now as we continue the Mass, may the Lord fill you with the peace and joy that only he can give as you prepare to celebrate the birth of his Son. Amen.

Feast of the Immaculate Conception
December 8, 2005

HOMILY – (Gen. 3:9-15, 20; Luke 1:26-38) The feast today is about Mary's conception, that from the instant she began to exist on this earth, indeed from her very conception, she was holy, filled with God's grace and without sin. The gospel today can confuse us somewhat because it tells us about Jesus' conception. It was read today, first of all, because there is no gospel telling us about the moment when Mary was conceived. And secondly today's gospel does give us an important piece of information about Mary related to today's feast. The angel greeted her as: "Full of grace." Our feast celebrates what the angel stated. There was no moment in Mary's life when God's grace did not fill her. She was full of grace.

As we listen in on this conversation between Mary and the Angel, we learn not only about Mary but also about the child she is going to have. Mary's son to be would be Son of the Most High and king forever. Her child will be called "holy, the Son of God." In the midst of all our business, we pause on this Holy Day to think what it is we are happy about at this time of year.

This is why Mary was "full of grace," so she could give birth to the source of all holiness and grace, God's own Son. And why did he come to us? So that we too can become holy. This is what St. Paul tells us in today's second reading: "God chose us in him to be holy and blameless in his sight."

Holiness is something few people strive for. All of us want to get to heaven, but most of us would probably tend to say I just want to get inside the door. We should do more than just try to get inside the door. We are called to be holy. Most of us never think that becoming holy is our vocation. We usually think holiness is for someone else, like the saints or people in religious orders. That's because we do not understand holiness. We think being holy means spending all day praying or wearing ourselves out doing good things for others and never having a chance to have any fun. I think holy people probably have as much fun as any of us, but there's something greater than fun. It is joy and peace and love. To be holy means to be close to God. The closer we are to God, the more we will be filled with love and joy and peace – both in this life and throughout eternity.

Our vocation to holiness is illustrated by the two stories we heard today.

The first story was about our first parents who originally were very close to God and were very happy.

That was the symbolism of the Garden of Eden. But that wasn't good enough for them. They wanted to be like God himself. So they rebelled against God and they lost all they had.

The second story, the Annunciation, illustrates Mary's constant attitude of being willing to say "yes" to God. It was only through her openness that the Son of the Most High has come to us. St. Luke tells us Mary was not only holy and always ready to do whatever God wanted of her, but he also tells us she was joyful. Holiness and joy are connected. After the angel left Mary, St. Luke told us about Mary visiting her cousin and she was full of joy. She expressed her joy in the beautiful hymn "the Magnificat." "My soul gives glory to the Lord and my spirit rejoices in God my savior."

In reflecting on the holiness of Mary, we may feel as if we were treated unfairly. We were born with original sin. The deck was stacked against us from the beginning. But we forget that when we were baptized we were filled with God's life. The very same grace that filled Mary at the moment of her conception, filled us when we were baptized. So holiness is possible for us too. Our two stories can show us there are two ways each of us can go in life. We can follow the example of our first parents, Adam and Eve, or we can follow the example of Mary. The first will lead to sorrow, the other to joy. To imitate Mary, all we have to do is say "yes" to whatever God asks of us.

3rd Sunday of Advent
December 16, 2012

INTRODUCTION – (Zephaniah 3:14-18a; Philippians 4:4-7; Luke 3:10-18) Our theme for today, as it often is, is summed up in the Psalm refrain: "Cry out with joy and gladness, for among you is the great and holy one of Israel." Our first reading from the prophet Zephaniah goes back about 700 years before Christ. The Assyrians were the dominant force in the Middle East at that time. They were an unusually warlike, brutal people. Their capital city was in northern Iraq near modern day Mosul. Our first reading comes from a time shortly after the Assyrians annihilated the northern part of Israel. They brought severe suffering upon the southern part of Israel too, the area around Jerusalem, but they did not conquer it. Jerusalem would still be around for another 130 years until the Babylonians conquered it. Yet in spite of the pain the Assyrians inflicted upon Jerusalem, the people did not learn from the prophets that they needed to obey God in order to prosper. Idolatry and immorality were rampant among the people of Jerusalem. For example, the king of Judah offered his own son as a human sacrifice to the pagan gods of the Canaanites. Most of what is written in the Book of Zephaniah records his efforts to correct abuses among God's people. Today we hear only the last part of the Book of Zephaniah as the prophet addresses those who are faithful to God. He tells them to rejoice and assures them God will rejoice and sing too because of his love for them and for all the blessings that will be theirs. Imagine how beautiful it would be to hear God singing.

There is something we should be aware of when we hear the second reading too. St. Paul is sitting in prison somewhere when he wrote this, and prisons in those days were really bad. Today's prisons would look like a five star hotel by comparison. Yet, even as he sits in prison, Paul can be joyful and he is able to encourage the Philippians to have no anxiety and to rejoice always.

HOMILY – In the days when we had Mass in Latin, this Sunday was known as Gaudete Sunday because the first word of the entrance hymn was Gaudete, a word that means "Be Joyful." The priest wears rose-colored vestments rather than the usual more somber colored violet vestments and today's readings tell us to rejoice. Friday evening, after finishing my homily, totally centered on the theme of joy, I decided to watch the news before I went to bed. The news wasn't very joyful as it reported on the tragic killing of 20 innocent children and 6 adults in Sandy Hook Elementary School in Connecticut earlier in the day. This horrible thing is beyond description. With thoughts of this tragedy still on my mind, it is with mixed feelings I begin my homily today. I am convinced it all comes down to "respect for life." In our world and in our country, respect for life continues to be eroded away. As it becomes less and less an ethical and moral value, there will always be people on the fringes of society who will push things even beyond any rational or civilized boundaries. We all feel sadness for those suffering from this terrible evil and we remember them in our prayers.

Fortunately there is more good in the world than there is evil, so, in spite of times of sadness and tragedy, we do have things about which we can be joyful, especially the birth of Jesus who came to bring us eternal joy. Joy is the theme for today because the celebration of Jesus' birth is so close.

We heard the prophet Zephaniah in today's first reading telling God's people, during an especially difficult time in their history, to "sing for joy." Why? Because God was in their midst. We heard Paul, even in prison, telling the Philippians to rejoice always. Paul makes it sound like it's something we are able to choose to do if we wish, and most of the time it is. There are things we can do to lift our spirits or there are things we do that pull us down and rob us of joy. I talk about some of those things such as self-pity, guilt, unforgiveness, anger, resentment, fear, and worry in my homily book on the third Sunday of Advent. That book is available at the doors of the church. Rather than repeating what I have said in the past, I would like to look at the gospel for a few thoughts. Last week we heard from John the Baptist who identified himself as a voice crying in the wilderness: "prepare the way of the Lord." The people asked, "what should we to do?" In other words: "how do we prepare?" We don't hear John's full message, but there is enough here to think about. It struck me that although John was a fire and brimstone prophet, his message tells us some important things about joy.

Look at the first thing he says: "whoever has two cloaks should share with the person who has none. He tells us this applies to food also. He's not talking about spreading the wealth, but he is talking about being sensitive to the basic needs of others. Reaching out a helping hand to a person in need gives us a sense of satisfaction, a feeling of joy. The opposite of helping others is greed, where we're only interested in helping ourselves. A greedy person is not a happy person, it is a person always wanting more. John says tax collectors should not try to gouge people for more than was prescribed. Tax collectors made their living on whatever they could squeeze out of people and most likely a lot of them tried to get all they could. That's partly why they were so despised. John told soldiers not to be bullies, to be honest and to be satisfied with their wages. That would not be a popular thing to preach about these days! Notice John has a message for tax collectors and soldiers, two groups who were despised by the Jews. It shows Luke's concern for those on the margins of society, a concern Jesus himself would have for the poor and for sinners. Greed is an assumption that the more we have the happier we will be. But that is a false assumption for, even though we do have material needs, our deepest longings will never be fulfilled with things. A greedy person, as I said, is always unsatisfied.

We do not yet fully have that which will fulfill our deepest needs, which is God. We have begun to enjoy God's presence and love through faith in Jesus, who has come to us, but as the letter of John the evangelist tells us, "what we shall be has not yet come to light. We do know that when it is revealed we shall be like him, for we shall see him as he is." (1 John 3:2) And so our life on earth now is a time of Advent as we wait and as we prepare for Jesus coming to us to lead us into the fullness of God's kingdom, a kingdom of joy. Amen.

4th Sunday of Advent
December 23, 2012

INTRODUCTION – (Micah 5:1-4a; Hebrews 10:5-10; Luke 1:39-45) In today's first reading the prophet Micah is speaking words of hope to God's people in Jerusalem during an attack by the Assyrians about 700 years before Christ. He promises salvation would come, and it would come out of an unimportant little village about seven miles south of Jerusalem named Bethlehem. Bethlehem had been the birthplace of King David 300 years before the prophet Micah. The greatness of the savior to come would reach to the ends of the earth. When the Magi came to Jerusalem looking for the newborn king of the Jews, 700 years later, this was the Scripture passage that guided them to where Jesus was. What an amazing prophecy; what an amazing way in which God fulfilled it!

HOMILY – St. Matthew and St. Luke tell us about

events that happened at the time of Jesus' birth. Matthew focuses mostly on St. Joseph and Luke focuses primarily on the Blessed Virgin.

Today's short gospel describes the visitation of Mary to her cousin Elizabeth. In reading today's gospel earlier this week, I asked myself why Luke was telling us this story. My homily helped answer that question for me; I hope what I discovered will be helpful to you in knowing Jesus and Mary better. Our gospel today takes place right after Luke's account of the Annunciation, the beautiful gospel where the angel Gabriel asked Mary if she would consent to be the mother of the Messiah. Mary could never say "no" to God. On that occasion Gabriel also told Mary that her much older relative, Elizabeth, had conceived and already was in her sixth month. The next thing Luke tells us is that Mary went in haste to be with her and that is the beginning of today's gospel. When I pray the rosary, I frequently reflect on Mary's eagerness to help her cousin. Mary could have been filled with pride knowing she was to be the mother of a son, a great person who would be called Son of the Most High and who would inherit the throne of King David, which no one had occupied for almost 600 years. She could have considered herself too important to help her aged relative, but she didn't. She went with haste. But possibly there is another reason for her haste. The angel Gabriel had told her that it was in God's plan for Elizabeth to have a child; it wasn't just an unplanned pregnancy. "Nothing is impossible for God," Gabriel said. Mary's haste is indicative of her enthusiastic obedience to participate in God's plan.

Luke is thus telling us something about Mary. Luke presents her to us as the example of the always faithful disciple. Once when Jesus was preaching, a woman in the crowd called out: "blessed is the womb that bore you and the breasts that nursed you." (only Luke tells us of this event - Luke, 11:27) and Jesus answered, "Rather blessed are those who hear the word of God and keep it." Jesus' answer tells us it is faith in God and doing what God wants that makes the ideal disciple. So when Elizabeth says to Mary: "Blessed are you who believed that what was spoken to you by the Lord would be fulfilled," Luke is putting Mary before us as the example of the always faithful disciple. This is the second time in today's short gospel that Elizabeth said Mary was blessed. The first time was when Elizabeth said: "blessed are you among women and blessed is the fruit of your womb," a phrase we repeat whenever we say the "hail Mary." The two blessings that Elizabeth speaks tell us that Mary is indeed twice blest, she is the physical mother of the Messiah and she is first and most faithful among Jesus' disciples. Mary's response to these praises coming from Elizabeth is to bless God for the gracious privilege God has given her. She prays the beautiful Magnificat which follows this gospel passage: "my soul proclaims the greatness of the Lord".

Luke is not only telling us about Mary, but this scene also reveals to us something about Jesus, something more than Gabriel told Mary in the Annunciation. In the Annunciation we learned that Jesus was conceived by the Holy Spirit. Now we learn that Jesus brings that Spirit to others. Luke tells us Elizabeth was filled with the Holy Spirit at the visit of Mary and Jesus. So was the unborn John the Baptist. Because Elizabeth was filled with the Spirit, she could interpret John's movement within her: he leaped for joy. The Spirit that brings us joy entered John at that moment too. Earlier Luke told us that when Gabriel appeared to Zachariah, John's father, that John "would be filled with the Holy Spirit even from his mother's womb." (Lk. 1:15). The gift of the Spirit on this occasion foreshadows Jesus' sending the Spirit on his disciples on Pentecost.

Another important statement about Jesus is in Elizabeth's question: "how does this happen that the mother of my Lord should come to me?" It is the same question that King David asked (1000 years earlier) when the Arc of the Covenant was brought into Jerusalem: "How can the ark of the Lord come to me?" (2 Sam. 6:9) The ark symbolized the presence of Israel's God among God's people. Mary's visit to Elizabeth blessed her home with the presence of God. As we prepare for Christmas we too ask ourselves that awesome question. And we are still unable to comprehend the profound answer we know to be true: "How does this happen that my Lord should come to me?" Amen.

Christmas
December 25, 2012

INTRODUCTION – In our first reading we hear from Isaiah the prophet who lived 700 years before Christ. The king who reigned at the time of Isaiah refused to trust in God and his policies brought darkness and gloom upon God's people. We hear Isaiah prophesy the birth of a king whose reign would bring peace and justice to God's people.

HOMILY – On Christmas morning, little five year old Tommy wasn't thrilled with the few toys and lots of clothes he had received. As he slowly trudged upstairs after opening his presents, his dad asked: "where are you going?" "To my room" he said, "to play with my new socks." (*Reader's Digest*: Dec. 2008, pg. 206)

As she prepared to wrap her Christmas presents, a mother discovered she didn't have any Christmas wrapping paper. The only wrapping paper she had said "Happy Birthday" on it. So she improvised. She got a big marking pen and wrote the word "Jesus" after "Happy Birthday." (*Reader's Digest*, Dec. 2012, pg 21)

In our first reading today, we heard the prophet Isaiah tell God's people that God would send them a king who would bring peace and justice to the people. He would not be like the king who was reigning at that time. It took 700 years before Isaiah's prophecy would come true. You would think that God's people would have forgotten about this prophecy, but they didn't. Their hope was still very much alive at the time of Jesus, waiting with high expectation for that Wonder-counselor, God-hero, father-forever and prince of peace, as Isaiah had foretold. Today we celebrate his birth.

He came to us in utter simplicity and humility, but the angels of God and the stars in the sky could not contain themselves. They had to announce his birth to everyone from those at the bottom of the social ladder, the shepherds, and to those whom society held in high esteem, the magi. Over two billion people in the world today celebrate his birth and praise God for the gift of Jesus.

Jesus didn't come just for us to make a big deal over his birth. He wants us to learn from his teachings, to imitate his example of love, to accept him as our savior and to find in him our hope. He wants us to spend eternity with him. We sometimes wonder where is that peace he came to bring, the love he taught, the eternal life he came to give. People still suffer, get sick, start wars, steal, cheat and kill. Where is the new life he came to bring us? First of all, we have to buy into his message to know his new life. Second, we have to realize that the peace he brings is not of this world, nor is his kingdom of this world. Only when we accept him fully into our lives does it all begin to make sense.

St. Luke and St. Matthew tell us very little about the birth itself, but St. Luke keeps us focused on the manger in which Jesus lay. Most commentators see a connection between the manger of Jesus and a statement in the beginning of the book of Isaiah. Isaiah told God's people, "Sons I have raised and reared, but they have disowned me! An ox knows its owner, and a donkey, its master's manger; but Israel does not know, my people has not understood." In other words, even a dumb animal knows who takes care of it and feeds it, but God's people did not know their God who took care of them. When the angel announced the birth of Jesus to the shepherds they went to find the baby Jesus in a manger. In other words, Luke is telling us God's people are beginning to find their God again in Jesus. And in finding him, God's people will be cared for and fed by him. Jesus himself tells us: "I am the bread of life." He feeds us and nourishes us with his word and with his love. He invites us to be at least as smart as an ox and a donkey who know who takes care of them and feeds them. (One other detail I might interject here: Bethlehem comes from two Hebrew words, which mean "the house of bread.") Jesus wants us to do more than make a big deal out of his birth; he wants us to come to him and to find our life and our inner strength in him. As he tells us, he is the way, the truth and the life.

I want to thank all of you who have come here today to celebrate Jesus coming to us. May he fill your hearts with joy, and may his love strengthen you all through the year. Amen.

Feast of the Holy Family
December 30, 2012

INTRODUCTION – (1 Samuel 1: 20-22, 24-28; 1 John 3:1-2, 21-24; Luke 2:41-52) Our first reading takes us back over 1000 years before Christ, just before there were kings in Israel. Hanna (the first person mentioned) was unable to conceive a child. If a woman in that culture could not conceive, it was looked upon as God's punishment for something. Her husband had two wives and the other wife used to taunt Hanna at every chance she could get. Hanna prayed very hard to be able to have a child. In her prayer she made an interesting promise. She promised that if she had a male child, she would dedicate the child to God and give him back to the service of God. She did have a child she named Samuel. Today's reading is the account of her returning Samuel back to God. She took him to where the Arc of the Covenant was kept, which was at Shiloh at the time, and entrusted him to the high priest, Eli, who would raise and educate and train Samuel in God's ways. Samuel became a great prophet and was the one who chose the first two kings of Israel: Saul and David. The story prepares us for the gospel of the finding of Jesus in the Temple at the age of twelve. When Jesus tells Mary he must be about his Father's business (or his Father's house, as it is often translated), I suspect Mary knew someday she would have to give Jesus back to God the Father.

HOMILY – As a husband and wife were dressing to go out for New Year's Eve, the wife asked her husband: "do you think this dress makes me look fat?" He said to her: "do you think this shirt makes me look stupid?"

A mother wrote in to *Reader's Digest* that the highlight of her trip to the zoo with her children was a peacock showing off its plumage. The four year old son was particularly taken with it and that evening when the dad came home he couldn't wait to tell his father: "Dad, guess what! I saw a Christmas tree come out of a chicken."

Overheard at the beauty parlor was a married woman complaining to her hair dresser about her husband. She said "things have gotten so bad, I'm thinking of getting a divorce. What do you think?" Her hair dresser replied: "that's a serious question. I don't think I'm qualified to give an opinion. You better consult another hair dresser." (from *Reader's Digest*: Dec. 2009/Jan. 2010, pg 188)

A wife sat down on the couch next to her husband who was flipping channels on the TV. She asked: "what's on the TV?" He said "dust!" Then the fight began.

One could go on for a long time with funny stories about families. If your family is not perfect, you're not alone. There are lots of dysfunctional families around. Some dysfunctions are tragic; others are just plain funny. I'll bet even the Holy Family, most likely the perfect family, had a few things happen in their relationships that gave them a few laughs. The story we hear today, the only event recorded about Jesus when he was growing up, was not funny at all. Joseph and Mary were in anguish. They must have thought that as parents they were irresponsible and awful failures.

Luke tells us the holy family went up to Jerusalem every year for the Passover - a seven or eight day event. In the Temple there was a section where the women prayed and worshipped and a different section for the men. Since Jesus was twelve years old, he could have stayed with Mary in the women's section or he could have stayed with Joseph in the men's section. At age 13 he would have been obligated to join the men. Not only did the men and women pray separately, they would gather together into groups (for safety) and they would travel separately. So apparently when Joseph and Mary returned to Galilee after Passover, they both assumed Jesus was in the group with the other parent. No one knows how it was that Jesus missed out on joining either group. Ann Rice, in her book: *Christ the Lord, Out of Egypt*, describes the possibility that on this particular visit to Jerusalem, Jesus found out from the scribes and Pharisees about the things that happened when he was born, the shepherds who found him, the magi who were looking for him, the killing of infant boys in Bethlehem by King Herod. He had inklings that he was somewhat different before this time, but someone among the Jewish elders told him about all the unusual things that happened at his birth and the whole revelation dumbfounded and exhausted him, so much so that he missed the caravan going back to Galilee. That whole description that Ann Rice gives us in her book is pure speculation, but it's one that makes sense to me. Behind this explanation is the assumption that Jesus did not have clear knowledge yet of who he really was. Some theologians think Jesus knew who he really was from the very beginning, while others believe it wasn't until Jesus was an adult that he knew he was Son of God. It's a debate that will never be answered in this life. I just gave you Ann Rice's explanation because she helps me imagine what might have happened.

Luke tells us even Mary and Joseph did not understand what he said to them as to why he had not joined them on the way back home. It shows the perfectly human side of the holy family; what family hasn't had to go through times of crisis. At the same time it implies the divine nature of Jesus. Whether Jesus' answer is translated "in my Father's business" or "in my

Father's house," the reference is to God and Jesus' very unique relationship with him. How blest we are that Jesus shares his special relationship with the Father with us by sharing God's life with us through grace and teaching us to pray to God as Our Father. Amen.

Mary, Mother of God
January 1, 2010

HOMILY – (Numbers 6:22-27; Galatians 4:4-7; Luke 2:16-21) I entertained myself this afternoon looking up information about the new year. I've always wondered how January 1 became New Year's Day. I wondered how other cultures celebrate New Year's. I've always known that the Jewish new year begins on Rosh Hashanah which will fall on September 18, 2009. I've always known that the Chinese have their own new year celebration which this year will be Jan. 26, 2009. Because their calendar is a little shorter than ours, the Moslems began two new years' in 2008; one in January and another in December. But I was amazed to see all the other cultures that have their own new year at different times and seasons. January 1 was chosen as the start of the new year by the early Romans in 153 BCE. Prior to that date they celebrated the new year in the spring which seems logical since nature starts to come alive at that time. But in 153 BCE the Roman senate chose January 1 as the beginning of a new year because that was the day when the Roman consuls took office. The date is quite arbitrary. It is said they celebrated with "boisterous joy, superstitious practices and gross orgies." The early Christians made January 1 a day of penance as a reaction against the excesses of the pagans. Eventually it was made a feast of Mary as the "Mother of God." I learned too that many European countries didn't officially make January 1 the start of the new year until the 16th, 17th, and 18th centuries. Now practically all big cities of the world celebrate January 1 even if they have their own new year, like China. The Church's celebration of the new year is the first Sunday of Advent. It makes little reference to January 1 as the start of a new year as it falls during the octave of Christmas. Christmas is too important a feast for just a one-day celebration, so the liturgy celebrates Christmas solemnly for eight days. After today, the liturgy continues to celebrate Christmas, but less solemnly, until the feast of the Baptism of our Lord. Although the angel had already told Joseph that Mary's son was to be named Jesus, today also recalls the day on which Jesus was circumcised and officially given his name. We might reflect for a moment how respectful we are of this name by which we are to be saved. Pope Paul VI asked that today be observed as a day of prayer for peace, which is so badly needed in today's world. As we celebrate the beginning of 2009 we are hopeful nations might find a better way than waging war to get along with one another. We are hopeful also that our world will be more just, that life will be respected, that we might enjoy health and happiness. Although we may party at this time of year, we also have a lot of reasons to be here in church, to seek God's help in the coming year, and to thank him for his help in the past. Mary, the Mother of God and our spiritual mother gives us an example of how to enter into this new year. We are told she reflected on all these events in her heart. What events? The annunciation by the angel, the visit to her cousin Elizabeth, Jesus' birth, the visit by the shepherds and the magi. May we too continue to reflect on them in our hearts. The rosary can help us in this. May we come to know God's support as we move another year closer to the kingdom of his eternal love. Amen.

Feast of the Epiphany
January 6, 2013

INTRODUCTION – (Isaiah 60:1-6; Ephesians 3:2-3a, 5-6; Matthew 2:1-12) 587 years before Christ, Jerusalem was destroyed by the Babylonians (modern day Iraq) and most of the Jews who lived in and around Jerusalem were taken to Babylon as exiles and slaves. Fifty years later, the Persians (people living in modern day Iran) conquered the Babylonians, and they allowed the Jews to return home. I can't possibly imagine the difficulties and stresses the Jewish people were under as they tried to rebuild their homes, their Temple, their farms after the Babylonians destroyed everything 50 years earlier. The prophet in today's first reading tries to encourage God's people and assure them Jerusalem would again be a great city. He sees Jerusalem becoming a light for the whole world. His vision is that the Jews would no longer be the only people to learn about God and to worship God, but people would come from all nations to visit Jerusalem to be nourished by God's word and to worship at God's holy temple. St. Matthew sees the vision of the prophet fulfilled in the birth of Jesus and the visit of the magi.

HOMILY – According to George Burns the secret of a good sermon is to have a good beginning and a good ending and to have the two as close together as possible. I do not promise that from now on my every sermon will fit this pattern, but I know you have been patiently listening to a lot of sermons in the past two weeks. Today I'll do my best to give you a good sermon according to George Burns.

On Christmas we celebrated the Son of God taking on our human nature (a mystery called the Incarnation). Today the heavenly bodies themselves proclaim to all the world that God is living among us in human form.

The word Epiphany comes from the Greek and means an appearance, a manifestation or a showing forth. The Greek Church celebrates Epiphany in a big way - it is their celebration of Christmas. The Roman Church (that is us), after celebrating Jesus' birth, tends to focus primarily on the coming of the magi after Christ is born. The news is getting out.

In antiquity it was a general belief that the stars and planets in some significant way announced the birth of a great person. Magi is the plural form for the Greek word Magus. A magus was a Persian or Babylonian wise man and priest who was expert in astrology, interpretation of dreams and who possessed various other magical or occult powers. The Scriptures do not tell us how many magi came, but they traveled some distance, somewhere between 500 and 1000 miles. Travel was dangerous in those days and not very comfortable. There is a delightful mini-opera (in English) named Amahl and the Night Visitors. The opera takes as its theme three magi (in the opera they are kings) losing their way in their search for Christ and stopping at the home of a poor mother and child to spend the night. I'm sure you found it delightful if you have ever had a chance to hear it or see it.

Reflecting on the theme of the magi's long journey from Iraq or Iran to Jerusalem, I thought of how we all are on a journey, whether we are aware of it or not, as we pass through this life. On this journey we encounter pleasant or unpleasant events and surprises. Sometimes it moves along happily, sometimes it gets very difficult, sometimes we meet wonderful people along the way and sometimes not, but day by day we keep moving. Whether that journey leads to Christ or not depends on us. As the magi found the Scriptures helpful in their travels, so those same Scriptures can and will guide us.

As I thought of the magi coming from a far distance to find Christ, I thought many people who come here are like the magi, for they come long distances: Centerville, Delhi, Colerain Township, West Chester, Fairfield, Loveland, Lawrenceberg IN, Ft. Thomas, KY., etc. I am grateful so many people come from so many places. If we didn't have you, we would be out of business. I hope and pray that St. Boniface will always be a place where you can find Christ.

Just a few days ago we started a new year. One author described the beginning of a new year as a book with 365 blank pages. Each day we fill one page with the story of our journey. I pray that when all 365 pages are filled, your story will be a good one, and it will be if you keep moving in the direction of Christ. Amen

Baptism of the Lord
January 13, 2013

INTRODUCTION – (Isaiah 40:1-5, 9-11; Titus 2:11-14; 3:4-7; Luke 3:15-16, 21-22) Surely many people must have pleased God greatly during the Old Testament period, people such as Abraham, Moses, the prophets. In the book of the prophet Isaiah, God speaks of someone as his servant with whom he is especially pleased. In these four lengthy passages, known as the servant songs, the servant is not identified. Perhaps the passages refer to someone who was alive at the time of the prophet, but what is amazing is that although they were written 500 years before Jesus was born, they describe Jesus perfectly. Today's first reading is part of the first servant song. It has been chosen as today's first reading because we hear echoes of it at Jesus' baptism as God says to Jesus: "with you I am well pleased."

HOMILY – Although Dec. 26 is the end of the Christmas season for many people, the Church's liturgical year extends the Christmas season to the Baptism of our Lord. Thus our crib is still in church. What does the Baptism of our Lord have to do with the Christmas season? The Baptism of our Lord is part of the Epiphany theme. Remember "epiphany" means appearance or manifestation. Last Sunday we celebrated God manifesting his Son to all nations by the visit of the magi. Today we celebrate God manifesting his Son to us as he begins his public ministry.

People often wonder why Jesus chose to be baptized. He was without sin and John the Baptist was baptizing people for the remission of sin. Even John found it strange that Jesus came to him for baptism. St. Matthew's gospel tells us John tried to prevent his asking for baptism by saying to him: "I need to be baptized by you, and yet you are coming to me?" (Mt. 3:14) Yet Jesus insisted on it.

Scholars too are puzzled by Jesus' baptism. Many have speculated that Jesus was initially a disciple of John. His baptism may have indicated his early association with John and Jesus seeing his baptism as a preparation for his own ministry. That is one possible explanation. Another that is offered by scholars is that Jesus may have received John's baptism as a form of support and acceptance of John's mission of calling for repentance in preparation for the coming messiah. When many people think of John's baptism, they think of it as essentially the same as our sacrament of baptism, but it is not. The two are miles apart. We just heard in today's gospel John say, "I baptize with water, he is the one who will baptize with the holy Spirit."

Jesus did not need to be baptized. He was as holy as

he could be. He was God's Son from all eternity and when he was conceived it was by the Holy Spirit. For us to be filled with God's life, we need to receive baptism. When we are conceived, we are given a share in the life of our father and mother. To share God's life, we must be born again or born from above. The Greek word άνωθεν (anothen) can mean again or from above. Jesus tells the Pharisee Nicodemus in the gospel: "no one can enter the kingdom of God without being born of water and Spirit." (Jn. 3:5) When we are baptized, we are at that moment made truly God's children and the Spirit fills us. When we are baptized, God whispers to each of us "you are my beloved child."

When we are conceived, we begin life as a human person; when we are baptized, we begin life as a child of God. We have a lot of growing to do in both arenas. As we grow, we learn who our parents are, how to love them and receive their love, how to communicate with them, how to obey them. As God's child, we learn that God is our Father, how to love God and how to receive God's love, how to communicate with God and how to obey God.

The child has its parents and the Church to guide him or her in learning how to live life in this world and how to prepare for life in the next. Baptism is thus not a one-time event that we can go through and then forget about. It sets our life on a path of holiness for this world and for eternity.

Jesus was baptized with the baptism of John at the beginning of his public ministry of preaching, healing and casting out demons. We are baptized with the baptism of Jesus to begin to live our life in the Spirit of Christ. May the events at Jesus' baptism inspire us to know who we are and to keep us growing in the right direction. Amen.

2nd Sunday in Ordinary Time
January 20, 2013

INTRODUCTION – (Isaiah 62:1-5; 1 Corinthians 12:4-11; John 2:1-11) For almost fifty years, the Jews were captives and exiles in Babylon (modern day Iraq). Then the Persians (modern day Iran) conquered the Babylonians, and they allowed God's people to return home. The Persians were even willing to give them financial aid to rebuild their Temple, their homes, their cities and their farms. The prophet in today's first reading announces this wonderful event that God would bring his people back home. During their exile, God had not forgotten his people and would take his people back to himself as his bride. The image of Israel as God's spouse is an important biblical image, found in several of the prophets, and is the best symbol from our human experience that can be used to describe the affection God has for us. This wedding image prepares the way for the gospel account of Jesus' first miracle at the wedding feast of Cana.

HOMILY – A man was just getting ready to step into the shower and his wife came into the bathroom to get her medicine. The husband asked her this off the wall question (maybe he was expecting some kind of a compliment as an answer): "what do you think the neighbors would say if I cut the grass dressed like this?" Giving him a casual glance, she replied, "They'd say I married you for your money." (*Reader's Digest: Laughter, the Best Medicine*, pg 178) Our gospel reading is about marriage and Jesus' first miracle at a wedding celebration (which I understand went on for several days in the culture of that time - not surprisingly the wine ran out.)

I want to connect this Sunday's gospel with two feasts

we've just celebrated. Two weeks ago we celebrated the feast of the Epiphany. As I said the last two Sundays, the word Epiphany means appearance or manifestation. On Epiphany we reflected on God's manifesting his Son to all the nations through the coming of the Magi. Last Sunday, the feast of the Baptism of our Lord, God manifested his Son at Jesus' baptism when the Holy Spirit descended on Jesus and a voice came from the heavens that said: "You are my beloved Son, with you I am well pleased." Today's miracle of changing water into wine fits into this theme. Jesus is manifest as a wonder worker in his first miracle, and his disciples began to believe in him. This is one theme we can see in today's gospel. When one reads from John's gospel, however, there are various levels of meaning we can find in one passage.

I would like to reflect on another theme that is central to today's gospel: the idea of "change." Jesus' life was all about change. He came to change the world, to teach us how to do a better job of loving God and loving one another. He changed people who were sick and made them well. He changed sinners by forgiving them and telling them to live good lives (sin no more). He changed people who were possessed and set them free from the demons that controlled them. In his first miracle, he changed water into wine and changed what would have been a failed celebration into a great party.

He continues to call us to change. When he began to preach, he called people to change their lives, to get their priorities straight, and to put God first. He continues to work miracles of change in the special meal he gave us the night before he died. He took bread and turned it into his body and changed wine into his blood.

When Jesus called people to change their lives, it didn't always happen. We have a free will to accept what God has spoken to us or to reject it. Every other time

Jesus told something to change, however, it always happened, whether he was changing a blind person into a person with sight, or a lame person into one who was ambulatory, or whether it was a storm on the sea that he told to calm down. Why do many people then not believe in the Eucharist? Because he said at the Last Supper as he handed the apostles bread: "this is my body," and likewise with the cup of wine: "this is my blood." We can believe that the bread and wine were truly changed when he said those sacred words. We just can't see it. I might add, we can't always believe what we see, but we can always believe what Jesus said.

This changed bread and wine that becomes Jesus' body and blood will change us. We will become more like him and grow closer to him. Our faith is not a static thing, it is dynamic because the power of Jesus is at work. Later on in John's gospel he tells us, "I came that they may have life, and have it to the full." I think this is one of the most powerful lines in the gospel. If we believe in him and if we let him, Jesus will keep changing us until we come to the fullness of life. Amen

3rd Sunday in Ordinary Time
January 27, 2013

INTRODUCTION – (Nehemiah 8:2-4a, 5-6, 8-10; 1 Corithians 12:12-30; Luke 1:1-4, 4:14-17) Almost 540 years before Christ the Persians (Iran) conquered Babylon (in Iraq) and the Persians allowed the Jewish exiles living in Babylon to return to Israel. However, after having lived in Babylon for fifty years, most of the Jews had made a home for themselves there and were quite comfortable where they were. Even a hundred years after being allowed to go back to Israel, those who returned were still struggling in their efforts to rebuild their farms and their cities. Today's first reading brings us back to that period, 100 years after the return and restoration had begun. The Persians were still in control of the Middle East. Today's first reading is from one of the historical books in the Old Testament, the book of Nehemiah. Nehemiah had an important position as a servant to the Persian king, Artaxerxes I. Aware of the difficulties the Jews were confronted with, the king allowed Nehemiah to return to Israel to help his people rebuild, and appointed Nehemiah to be governor in Israel. In an effort to rebuild the Jewish nation, Nehemiah focused his efforts of rebuilding on what was most important, and that was their faith in God. In today's first reading Nehemiah called for a general assembly of the people and he delegated the priest-scribe, Ezra, to read God's word to them. Being a scribe, Ezra would have been one of the few people who know how to read and write. Being a priest, he could publicly expound on the meaning of the Scriptures. So Ezra read God's word to the people and interpreted it for them. The reading was most probably from the first five books of the Bible. Notice how the people actively responded to God's word. Jesus reads God's word to his former neighbors in Nazareth in today's gospel, but he gets mixed results.

HOMILY – These first verses of Luke's gospel (ch. 1) are important for he describes why he was writing it and the care he had taken to compose it. These four verses are followed immediately by a section called the Infancy Narrative, where Luke tells the story of the annunciation and birth of John the Baptist and of Jesus. The section of the Infancy Narratives is read during Advent and Christmas. It is followed by the Baptism of Jesus and Jesus' temptation in the wilderness. The next part of Luke's gospel brings us today's gospel in Chapter 4, the beginning of Jesus' public ministry.

Luke introduces Jesus' public ministry with a general statement that Jesus was going around Galilee teaching and his teaching was creating a reputation for Jesus. Luke doesn't mention the miracles Jesus had been working or what Jesus had been teaching. Instead he brings us to the visit Jesus made to Nazareth, the place where he grew up and lived for most of his life, until he was about 30 years old. This is an important episode in Luke's gospel because it foreshadows the entire ministry of Jesus that Luke is going to tell us about: that is, Jesus' early ministry that led first to his popularity and then eventually to his rejection.

Did you notice these few words where Luke tells us Jesus went into the Synagogue on the Sabbath, "as was his custom." Jesus was still going to church faithfully. It's not always so important for people today, even those who are Catholics. We've all seen these bumper stickers that say, "what would Jesus do?" That statement kind of bugs me because Jesus would often say or do surprising things. But one thing St. Luke wants us to know is that Jesus faithfully practiced his religion. St. Luke told us this same thing earlier in his gospel when he told us about the Holy Family going up to the Temple when Jesus was twelve years old. Luke said: "now every year his parents went to Jerusalem for the festival of the Passover." Passover was a week-long celebration with two or three days travel time going and two or three days travel time getting home. Worship was a high priority in the life of Jesus.

In a typical synagogue liturgy, the people would have heard a passage from the Pentateuch (the first five books of the bible) and a passage from the prophets with a reflection after each. Jesus was invited to do the second reading, which he apparently chose himself, from Isaiah. The passage in Isaiah describes God restoring his people to Israel after the Babylonian exile. God's word is always sacred, but on this occasion Jesus is telling his listeners that what he is about to say is an especially sacred moment, "today this Scripture passage is fulfilled in your hearing." In other words, what Isaiah said 500 years earlier would find an even greater fulfillment in what Jesus had to say. Through Jesus, God is bringing salvation to God's people, especially the poor, prisoners (most likely those who couldn't pay off their debts), the blind and the downtrodden. Scripture scholars all point out that the Isaiah passage adds that God would take vengeance on the enemies of his people; i.e., the Gentiles. In reading from Isaiah, Jesus omitted that phrase. It was salvation he had come to announce, not vengeance, and it would be a salvation offered to the entire world, to all nations.

Jesus saw himself as being guided by the Spirit (the Spirit of the Lord is upon me). Now in the Spirit he proclaims the good news of God's saving love. He was an immediate success. For a moment I'm going to get ahead of myself and refer to next Sunday's gospel. Apparently his hearers, who knew him as a child and later as a simple craftsman, wanted some kind of a sign from him for he said to them: you are probably saying to yourselves: "do here in your own country what we have heard you have been doing in Capernaum." Then they turned on him and were ready to kill him. He walked away from them, however, for his good work had to go on until it was the right moment. When that moment arrived, he would give up his life rather than discontinue his ministry and he would rise again and continue his work through the Spirit and through the Church. We are invited to be part of that sacred moment each time we are at Mass. Amen.

4th Sunday in Ordinary Time
January 31, 2010

INTRODUCTION – (Jeremiah 1:4-5, 17-19; 1 Corinthians 12:31-13:13; Luke 4:21-30) As St. Luke begins his gospel, he tells **why** he wrote it and **how** he went about it. We heard that last week. Then he goes on to tell us the beautiful stories about the birth of John the Baptist and Jesus and about how Jesus was lost in the Temple when he was twelve years old. We are not told what else happened to Jesus as he was growing up. Since it was the custom in those days, we can only assume that he worked with his father as a craftsman. About the age of thirty, Jesus was baptized by John in the Jordan then was led by the Spirit into the desert to fast and pray for 40 days. Luke then begins to tell us about Jesus' ministry of teaching and healing and his visit to his hometown of Nazareth. As a devout person, Jesus went to the synagogue faithfully on the Sabbath and was invited to do a reading from the prophet Isaiah and teach on it. This is where last Sunday's gospel ended. Today we hear how his relatives and former neighbors responded to his message – with enthusiasm at first, but it turned into hostility. Our first reading, as usual, prepares us for the gospel. Jeremiah the prophet heard God's call to preach, a job that God warned him would lead to suffering and rejection.

HOMILY – Overheard in a restaurant: a lady was telling her friend, "my husband and I had a big argument and we ended up not talking to one another for three days. Finally, on the third day he asked where one of his shirts was. I said 'So, now you're talking to me.' He looked confused and asked 'What are you talking about?' I said, 'haven't you noticed I haven't spoken to you for three days?' He said: 'No, I just thought we were getting along.'" (from *Reader's Digest, Laughter – the Best Medicine*) Such is the joy and complexity of love. I'll say something about that later. But first, today's gospel. We are left with a lot of questions. How is it that Jesus' visit to his hometown turned from enthusiasm to such hostility they wanted to kill him? Or how did he get away from them without being harmed? Is Luke telling us, in summarized form, what took place over the course of a number of visits Jesus made to Nazareth as he began his ministry? Luke doesn't answer our concerns. The only detail he gives us is that the people didn't consider Jesus anyone special – even though they were already familiar with stories of his miraculous powers. I think St. Luke is giving us a warning of what was ahead for Jesus: how his ministry of teaching and healing started out to be very popular with the people. Gradually, as people, especially some of the Jewish leaders, really started to understand his message, opposition to him grew until he was put to death. Perhaps Luke is teaching us that we can't take Jesus on our terms but on his terms; we can't make Jesus into who we would like him to be. We must accept him on the basis of who he wants us to be. Perhaps Luke is also showing us that Jesus was not a politician who tried to cater to people's wants; he was a prophet who would be faithful to the mission God sent him on, no matter what the consequences were.

Our second reading from St. Paul is one of the most beautiful passages written by him. It is especially popular at weddings, and rightly so. It may sound romantic, and indeed a couple who loves one another in the way Paul describes love would surely not lose the romance in their relationship. But the love Paul talks about does not happen easily or without effort. It demands discipline, unselfishness and self-sacrifice. As Paul says, love is not self-seeking; he insists that without love we are nothing.

Paul means this literally. His argument for this statement comes one chapter earlier in his letter when he compares the Christian Community to the body of Christ. We are all a part of that body and none of us can say we can get along without the other members of the body. It's like our own body. It has many parts, and each part functions because it is part of the whole. If our arm were cut off it may have the appearance of an arm, but literally it would not be an arm. It would be a mass of bone and skin and flesh. It's only an arm when it is connected to the body, which gives it its life and it's ability to function. Without its connection to the body, it is nothing. What connects us with one another and makes us one body is love. Without love we are separate individuals, no longer one with our head, which is Christ, and no longer one with each other. Thus he argues that even if any of us were miracle workers and had all kinds of spiritual gifts, without love we are nothing. The word Paul uses for love (agape) is not the kind of love that seeks some kind of reward from the one we love (i.e., it is not based on what we can get out of a relationship). Agape is a giving kind of love, the kind of love that Jesus has for us. St. John tells us: "God is love (agape)," (1 John 4:8) so if we're without love we're without God and vice versa. Without being connected with God, we're not connected to the head or to the rest of the body.

Our Mass helps us to abide in his love. We listen to his words, we recall his sacrifice on the cross for us, and we are united with him, the source of all love (agape), in Communion. We ask his help though our prayers and we give thanks for his love for us. Don't forget (eucharistia) is the Greek word for giving thanks and that's what we are doing now.

5th Sunday in Ordinary Time
February 7, 2010

INTRODUCTION – (Isaiah 6:1-2a, 3-8; 1 Corinthians 15:1-11; Luke 5:1-11) Our first reading is one of my favorite Old Testament readings. It is from the prophet Isaiah who lived about 725 years before Christ. He describes his call from God to be a prophet. The setting is in Jerusalem in the Temple. Notice he is unable to describe what God looks like. He describes God's royal robe, the angels, the sounds and the profound sense of God's holiness. In this experience he becomes aware of his own unworthiness. You will recognize in this passage the inspiration for two familiar hymns: the Holy, Holy, which we say or sing at every Mass and the hymn, Here I Am, Lord.

In the other two readings we hear how two other people experienced God in Jesus Christ: Paul in his vision of the Risen Christ and Peter in the miraculous catch of fish.

HOMILY – Several years ago, Rabbi Joseph Telushkin wrote a little book called *Jewish Humor: What the Best Jewish Jokes Say about the Jews.* In it he tells this story: A man takes some very fine material to a tailor and asks the tailor to make him a pair of pants. He goes back a week later, but the pants are not ready. Two weeks go by, and still the pants are not ready. Finally, after six weeks, the pants are ready. The man tries them, and they fit perfectly. As he pays for them, he says to the tailor, "It took God only six days to make the world. And it took you six weeks to make just one pair of pants." "Yes," said the tailor, "but look at the pair of pants (perfect!) and look at the world (it's a mess)." The tailor was hinting that perhaps God would have done a better job if he weren't in so much of a hurry.

I wonder if the tailor ever read his bible. It tells us from the very beginning all that God made was good. God, moreover, put his human creatures in the garden of Eden, a paradise that would be a source of every delight. But God's first human creatures rebelled against God and destroyed the harmony and joy God had blessed them with. Somehow we, the children of those first humans, continue to follow their example. So if the world is in a mess, the bible is telling us, don't blame God. We humans have created that mess ourselves. Maybe God really didn't create the world in six days. After all the bible is not trying to teach science. It's trying to tell us that God made all things, not how. You may have heard the story that after God made Adam, and Adam was in the Garden of Eden for a while, God asked Adam how things were going. Adam told God he was enjoying everything, but he felt something was missing. God said, how about if I create a companion for you, someone you can put your arms around, someone who will laugh at your jokes, listen to your stories, who will give you no hassle and will cater to your every whim. Adam thought that would be great. God said it will cost you an arm and a leg. Adam thought for a few moments, then asked God, what can I get for a rib.

We know there is a lot of symbolism in the two creation accounts of Genesis. For example, men are not going around with a rib missing. The six days of creation is also symbolic. Scholars tell us this account of creation was written by a priest who was trying to teach his people, among other things, that they were to keep holy the Sabbath. Even God rested on the Sabbath. Actually God doesn't get tired and his work of creation is ongoing. Astronomy has discovered that new stars are forming all the time. New human beings are coming into the world all the time. Even Jesus told the Jewish leaders after one of his miracles: "My father is at work until now, so I am at work." (Jn 5:7). We heard how God is at work making the world better through his prophet, Isaiah. God appeared to Isaiah, and purified his lips so that he could proclaim God's message to God's people. God was at work through St. Paul in today's second reading proclaiming the resurrection. I would like to expand on this passage a little more. Paul's letter is one of the earliest writings in the New Testament, written about the year 56 or 57 (about 14 years before the first gospel was written), thus it is a very important testimony to the faith of the early Church. The Corinthians were having a problem accepting the idea of the resurrection of the body. They thought our body came back to life with the same problems, weaknesses, and flaws it had before we died. They thought their spirits would be freer without their bodies. That's not so, Paul said. He tells them "what I handed on to you, as of first importance, I also received." Because it is such an important doctrine, Paul dedicated the whole last part of his letter to the resurrection. Notice the kind of language he uses to indicate this is the Tradition of the Church: "I handed on to you what I also received." That is, this is what the Church always believed about Jesus, that although he was put to death, his body now lives and he is seated at the right hand of God the Father. Paul goes on (beyond today's passage) to explain how we too shall rise to new life with him. It is a new world God is creating, in the risen Lord Jesus. That's where our gospel comes in: Peter and the apostles, who were among the many who visibly saw Jesus after his resurrection, would now be catching people, Jesus told Peter. They would be bringing people into God's perfect Kingdom, leading them though baptism and the Eucharist to a new life, eternal life, where there would be no more pain or suffering or even death.

When we look around and see that the world is in terrible shape, let us not lose hope. God hasn't abandoned us, rather God continues to send people who will help to establish his eternal Kingdom, people like Isaiah, people like Paul, people like Peter and the apostles, people like you and me. Amen.

1st Sunday of Lent
February 17, 2013

INTRODUCTION – (Deut. 26:4-10; Romans 10:8-13; Luke 4:1-13) In our first reading from Deuteronomy, we hear Moses instructing the people in the proper way to worship God. They were to bring to the priest one tenth of the fruits of their land (aka: "tithing"). Along with their offering, they would acknowledge they were once a people without freedom or land. They were now to bring their offering in gratitude for all the ways God has blessed them. The reading prepares us for the gospel where the devil tries to tempt Jesus into worshipping him. The devil promises he in return would give Jesus power over all earthly kingdoms. Jesus quotes another part of Deuteronomy which says, "You shall worship the Lord your God and him alone shall you serve." (Deut. 6:13)

HOMILY – Five weeks ago we celebrated the baptism of Jesus by John the Baptist at the Jordan river. Since then we've heard about events that happened early on in Jesus' ministry, such as his first miracle at the wedding feast at Cana. Today we back track a little, to hear what happened right after Jesus' baptism. When Jesus was baptized, the Holy Spirit came down upon him and God proclaimed that he was well pleased with Jesus, his Son. Suddenly, as we just heard in the gospel, the scene changed dramatically. The Spirit that came down on

Jesus at his baptism led him into the desert. This dramatic shift tells us a lot about the dramatic ups and downs in our own spiritual journey. I trust most of you can remember times when you felt close to God as a loving Father, or you felt some special consolation. Without warning you felt as if you were in a spiritual desert. Suddenly God seemed far away, he seemed to be ignoring you and, as it were, hiding his face from you. Many saints I've read about have had experiences like this. In this desert a person often feels they've done something wrong, and God is angry. They don't realize these ups and downs are part of everyone's spiritual journey, including Jesus himself, and that it's during those desert periods our faith will be growing deeper and stronger if we don't give up or get discouraged. Thinking about the experience of Jesus has always been comforting to me when I feel as if I'm in a desert. Those desert times make us more vulnerable to temptation too. It's easy to pray and to love God when we feel that he's close to us and it's harder when he feels far away. Luke tells us in today's gospel that it was only after Jesus had fasted those 40 days that the devil showed up. In other words, Jesus was at his most vulnerable point, at least physically. So the devil suggested Jesus turn stones into bread to satisfy his hunger; he offered Jesus power and control over all earthly kingdoms; and, finally, the devil told him that he should come floating down from the peak of the Temple and the Jewish people would instantly recognize him as their messiah. These temptations, at first, seem so strange. They appear to be quite different from the run of the mill temptations most of us have to deal with: pride, lust, greed, envy, anger, etc., but in some ways our temptations are similar to those of Jesus. Basically, Jesus' temptations involved the possibility of his using his divine powers for his own benefit. I would suspect temptations like these continued to suggest themselves to Jesus throughout his entire life. For example, we might remember how after he had fed the people miraculously, they wanted to make him their king. He may have found that tempting, but we know he turned away from that possibility. Remember too how when he was arrested in the garden of Gethsemane, he said: "don't you know that I could call on my Father for help and at once he would send me more than twelve armies of angels?" (Mt. 26:53) Yet he would not call on his supernatural powers to save himself. Jesus came to serve and we see him time and time again using his unique powers to serve others, not himself. In this, the temptations of Jesus are similar to some of our own. Jesus has given us an example that when God has blessed us, we should not be greedy and selfish with what we've been given in terms of time, talent and treasure, but we should be willing to help others. Now, my last thought, I do not say to those who are already perfect. If you are already perfect you can tune me out, but if there is some room in your spiritual life for improvement, then I have one last word about temptation. During Lent we are encouraged to do something that will bring us closer to Christ or to give up doing something that may keep us from serving Christ more wholeheartedly. Whenever I decide to do something special for Lent, after a couple of weeks I discover that 40 days is a long time, and I begin to let my good intentions slip by the wayside. That's one of my temptations during Lent. I think it's true of others, that many people begin Lent with good intentions, but then get tired of doing what they promised themselves they would try to do better. You will be blessed greatly if you persevere. I say this not just to encourage you, but I say this to myself as well: "don't quit the good work you planned on doing for Lent." Amen.

2nd Sunday of Lent
March 4, 2007

INTRODUCTION – (Gen 15:5-12, 17-18; Phil 3:17-4:1; Luke 9:28b-36) Almost 4000 years ago, God made awesome promises to a man named Abram about how he would inherit much land, would have so many descendants they could not be counted, even how the whole world would be blessed through him. Abram had no evidence that these promises would ever be fulfilled. He asked God for some assurance that they would. So God gave Abram a special sign. It may seem complicated to us but it would have been easily understood by Abram. It was the way people made covenants or contracts in those days. The ritual of cutting an animal in half and walking between the halves was a symbolic way of saying "may the same thing happen to me as to this animal if I am unfaithful to my word." God is often represented as fire, and in this experience only God moved in-between the two halves of the animals. This indicated that God was not asking Abram to promise anything. God asked only for Abram's trust.

HOMILY – As our lives move along, there are disappointments but there are also hopes and promises that we look forward to. Abram (later named Abraham) looked forward to the promise of land, many descendants and numerous blessings. In an ecstatic experience God assured him his hopes would be fulfilled.

Jesus had several times warned his apostles that he would suffer and die. Now he gave three of them a special experience to help them know what was ahead, that his death would lead to glory. It was a glory so wonderful that they didn't want it to stop. They wanted to set up tents on the mountain, not for themselves but for Jesus, Moses and Elijah, and they wanted to stay there indefinitely. But it wasn't to be. They still had to go through challenging and difficult times before they came to the glory they had seen. Matthew and Mark leave us in the dark regarding what Jesus was talking about with Moses and Elijah, but Luke tells us they were talking about Jesus' departure from this world by his death in Jerusalem. That departure is translated here by the word "exodus." Jesus had to leave this world to enter into the glory that was ahead. Luke has thus allowed us to see there is a definite connection between the transfiguration and Jesus' passion. Perhaps the experience of the transfiguration was meant to give strength and hope to Peter, James, and John, to help them survive Jesus' arrest and crucifixion. Perhaps it was a gift from God the Father to Jesus to help bolster his commitment to be faithful to his mission. Whatever it was, it was a promise of future glory and an assurance that God would not let down those who trusted in him.

When Peter wanted to put up three tents for Jesus, Moses and Elijah, it is always understood that he was enjoying this ecstatic experience and didn't want it to end, and this is true. But I wonder whether Peter, in his way of thinking, was making Jesus equal to Moses and Elijah. He said: "Let us make three tents," as if Jesus were a great leader on a par with Moses and Elijah. God the Father's words: "This is my chosen Son" let the apostles know that Moses and Elijah were great men and great prophets, but Jesus is God's Son and no one could ever be on the same level with him.

If the transfiguration is a promise of future glory for Jesus and the Apostles, St. Paul gives us a promise of future glory for us when he tells us today "our citizenship is in heaven." We are only tourists in this world and it's not our true home. We must always have our bags packed because we never know when we will be called to move on. And we will be called. Paul tells us God "will change our lowly bodies to conform with his glorified body." We will be transfigured also. Lent helps us remember to be ready to move on and to make any changes in our lives we need to make, so we will be ready to meet our God in eternal glory.

Mass is always an assurance and a promise of what's ahead, especially in Communion. The consecrated bread and wine are Jesus' body and blood. We are reminded of his death for us. We are also assured that he hasn't left us orphans, but he is still with us and in Communion he wants us to be more closely united with himself. Someday we will enjoy perfect union when we will not have to experience him through signs and sacraments. We will know him directly and intimately. When we come to that stage, like the three apostles at the transfiguration, we won't ever want to leave. Unlike the apostles, we won't have to.

3rd Sunday of Lent
March 11, 2007

INTRODUCTION – (Exod 3:1-8a, 13-15; 1 Corinthians 10:1-6, 10-12; Luke 13:1-9) Our psalm refrain, "The Lord is kind and merciful," describes our theme for today. We hear about God's desire to bring his people, suffering as slaves in Egypt, into freedom. He chooses Moses to be the one to demand and obtain their freedom. Moses wasn't happy to have to do this. He had escaped from Egypt himself because he had killed an Egyptian who had attacked an Israelite. Now God tells him he has to go back and deal with the Egyptian king. God gives Moses a special gift, God's name: "Yahweh," translated as "I AM." What is so special about that? It was like giving someone your private phone number. God was assuring Moses of a special relationship Moses would have with him and letting Moses know he could call on God whenever he needed him.

In our second reading Paul reminds us of how many blessings and marvels God's people experienced as God led them through the desert to the Promised Land. But in spite of all the wonderful things God gave them, they were unable to enter into the Promised Land. In the end they had failed to continue trusting in God. He tells us not to be like them.

The theme that "the Lord is kind and merciful" shows up again in the gospel in a short parable about a fig tree. It was given opportunities of every kind to produce fruit, but it failed to do so. "The Lord is kind and merciful," but he expects us not to take his mercy for granted. With the help of his kindness, he expects us to grow in goodness and holiness.

HOMILY – A young girl brought her boyfriend home to meet her parents. The parents couldn't find many good qualities about him. When the parents had the opportunity to talk to their daughter later, by herself, the girl's mother said: "Dear, he doesn't seem like a very nice person." "Mom," the daughter answered, "if he wasn't nice, why would he be doing 500 hours of community service?" It's stretching things a bit to say "community service" fits into the theme of today's liturgy, but our readings remind us not to be like the fig tree in Jesus' parable today. We are to produce good works. God didn't create us just to take up space in this world. He wants more from us than that. He wants us to trust him, to love him and to do good for others.

I said in my introduction that the theme for today is "the Lord is kind and merciful." He is kind and merciful in many ways. One of the ways he is kind and merciful is in calling us to repentance and renewal. In the book of Revelation Jesus said: "Whoever is dear to me I reprove and chastise. Be earnest about it, therefore. Repent! Here I stand, knocking at the door. If anyone hears me calling and opens the door, I will enter his house and have supper with him, and he with me." This assumes that we all have room for improvement. God asks that of us and he also gives us the help we need to be better. That is kindness to us. He would not be kind if he didn't stimulate us to keep improving ourselves. The fact that he challenges us to change comes from his love as a caring parent. The parable of the fig tree is a call to live a positive life according to the gospel – doing good by loving God and others.

The conversation Jesus had about tragic events at the beginning of today's gospel was interesting. Sometimes people think when something bad happens to someone it is God's punishment. Jesus said that's not always true. He does not try to explain suffering here, but he is telling us not to be complacent, which we sometimes are. We can't think "well, if nothing bad is happening to me, it must be because I am so good." He tells us we all need to repent, i.e., to work to be better than we are. This season of Lent keeps reminding us of our need to grow in holiness and goodness. Many people I have talked with do nothing special during Lent. They think they're good enough. Others start off Lent with a great deal of enthusiasm praying more, making sacrifices or doing good work. But as the weeks drag on, they ease up with their good resolutions. We still have four more weeks of Lent. Our readings today are encouraging us to do what we can so we can come to Easter with mind and heart renewed.

Today we have the first of three Scrutinies. Our community prays for those who are preparing to come into the Church at Easter so that they are better able to live the Christian way of life. May we all do a better job of living up to what God wants of us. We must remember, though, at all times, whether God is comforting us, forgiving us, healing us, blessing us, encouraging us or correcting us, "The Lord is kind and merciful."

4th Sunday of Lent
March 18, 2007

HOMILY – (Josh 5:9a, 10-12; 2 Cor 5:17-21; Luke 15:1-3, 11-32) We just heard the story of a young boy whose life was misdirected by love of riches and pleasure. After his so called friends abandoned him and he suffered hunger and want for a period of time, he came to his senses and returned to his father. He returned a changed person. Fortunately, he had a loving and forgiving father who accepted him unconditionally. The point of the story is abundantly clear when we consider the relationship between the father and his younger son. As regards the relationship between the father and the older son, Jesus leaves the conclusion open-ended. We have to reflect on what might have happened, whether the older son gave in to his father's pleading to be forgiving or whether he refused. How we end the story will tell us a lot about ourselves.

I want to tell you about another young man whose story is somewhat similar. He was Catholic to start with but admits that he was not a very good one. His father was a government official and this young man enjoyed the comforts of those who were well off. He described himself at sixteen as a scatterbrained youth who had "turned away from God and did not keep his command- ments." As his story goes, he was kidnapped and sold as a slave and made to labor on a farm for six years. Like the prodigal son who was without friends and who suffered without adequate food or shelter, this young man came to his senses and he learned obedience through what he suffered. He discovered (and we quote) "God showed me how to have faith in him forever, as one who is never to be doubted." After six years God spoke to him in a way that he heard with his own ears. He would escape and God audibly told him when to leave and what direction to go in order to accomplish his escape. Miraculously God protected him along the way until he arrived back home. Like the prodigal son, he came home a new person. Although his parents wanted to keep him at home with them, his love for God led him to want to serve God as a priest. Even more than serving as a priest, his love for others led him to want to return to the people who captured and enslaved him and teach them about God. And that he did. After overcoming many obstacles, including rejection by the hierarchy, a breach of confidence by a friend to whom he entrusted a confession of his past life, his lack of education and social graces, he returned as a bishop to the people who had enslaved him. Once he arrived he wasn't greeted with open arms. Again, in his own words, he said "daily I expect either murder, or robbery, or enslavement." He writes elsewhere "they seized me with my companions. And on that day they most eagerly desired to kill me; but my time had not yet come. And everything they found with us they plundered, and myself they bound in chains." He feared nothing, for even if he were to be put to death, he felt that would have been the supreme act of love for his God. But God had other intentions than that he should be a martyr. For 30 years he served God and the people who once enslaved him and his work was blessed. He ordained many bishops and priests, established convents, monasteries and schools and in thirty years saw the conversion of almost all of Ireland. And of course you all know I've been talking about St. Patrick, who is one of our patronal saints and whose statue is under the choir loft. His work was so successful that in a short time Ireland was sending out missionaries to revitalize the faith of Europe which had fallen into decline. Irish missionaries have been a blessing to the Church ever since.

For those who are Irish and who honor Patrick, the best way to truly honor him is not by drinking a Guinness. We should respond to his example and his call to holiness. Again quoting Patrick, he asks those who believe in him and love him to "strengthen and confirm your faith...That will be my glory, for a wise son is the glory of his father."

And for those who are not Irish and who think too much is made of St. Patrick on March 17th, I would like you to think of how our faith has been strengthened by the witness of many Irish saints and how our civilization has been preserved by the scholarship of the Irish during the days when mainland Europe was being overrun by barbarians. The great heritage of western civilization, from the Greek and Roman classics to Jewish and Christian works, would have been utterly lost were it not for the holy men and women of unconquered Ireland. These Irish recorded the great works of western civilization in their monasteries and convents (remember all books had to be written by hand). They brought this learning back to Europe after it began to stabilize in the eighth century under Charlemagne. Whether you're Irish or not, we all owe a great debt to the Irish and we pray that our patron, St. Patrick, blesses our parish and our families.

5th Sunday of Lent
March 17, 2013

INTRODUCTION – (Isaiah 43:6-21; Philippians 3:8-14; John 8:1-11) God's people were a captive people, enslaved by the Babylonians 600 years before Christ. After 50 years of captivity, God sent them a prophet to announce to them that they were about to be set free. We hear that prophet in today's first reading. God tells them their release from the Babylonians would be no less spectacular than their release from slavery in Egypt centuries earlier. Even as the prophet speaks, he tells them the road back to their own land is being made ready. God's statement, "see, I am doing something new," leads us into the gospel. There we hear about a woman caught in adultery who was about to be sentenced to death. Jesus is doing something new: offering forgiveness rather than condemnation.

HOMILY – One afternoon the parish priest was getting ready to hear confessions. As he entered the confessional room, which had a divider in it, he found a man already in the room waiting for him. The man told the parish priest, "It's been 45 years since I've been to confession. I am impressed how things have changed. The room is well lit, it's a nice easy chair to sit in, a bottle of scotch, some nice cigars. It wasn't that way the last time I went." The parish priest said, "yes, it is rather comfortable, but where you are sitting is my side of the confessional room." By the way, if anyone wants to check out our confessional, they are welcome to. It's pretty simple.

I thought I might say something about confession today. The sacrament referred to as "confession" is also called the sacrament of penance or reconciliation. I thought the topic might be appropriate because of today's gospel where Jesus, as he had done many times in the gospels, demonstrates God's merciful love.

He did not come to condemn but to save. In the old days, which many of us remember, the priest often thought his job was to scold the penitent. Many people never came back because of that. I always tell our people in the RCIA, if a priest starts to bawl you out, get up and leave. Go to someone else who sees their role as that of Christ who offers freedom from guilt and shame and a sense of God's peace. Fortunately, I was blest with that kind of a confessor almost all my life. I've always felt that scolding doesn't help them to grow spiritually, but offering a person the chance to start over and the opportunity to know God's love does help a person to grow. Imagine how this woman in the gospel was changed by her encounter with Christ.

Jesus came not to condemn but to save. That's the purpose of confession or reconciliation. Sometimes the priest tries to guide a person to see how wrong their behavior might be, but that guidance should be done in a gentle and loving way. The only time I know that Jesus was ever harsh with anyone was with the religious leaders who thought they were perfect and refused to see their faults. We're all sinners. We are all in need of God's mercy and love. That's why Christ came to us. You'll notice when the chips were down and Jesus started writing on the ground, no one threw any stones. They knew he had called their bluff. Some people have speculated that Jesus was writing people's sins, but no one knows for sure. Anyway, we're all in the same boat with the crowd in the gospel, we would all have to walk away if Jesus said, "let the one among you who is without sin cast the first stone at her." Jesus does not whitewash sin or ignore the seriousness of it. More than anyone he knows how it hurts us and hurts our relationship with God. Notice he told the woman, "go and from now on, do not sin any more." The old catechism called this "a firm purpose of amendment."

In the first five or six centuries of the Church, people were allowed to receive confession only once in their lifetime. It was only for publicly committed serious sins. The attitude of Church leaders was that if a person sinned again, there was no hope for them. In addition, people had to go through a period of public penance before reconciliation. Around the sixth or seventh century, mostly due to the influence of the monasteries, a practice developed where the sacrament began to be used as spiritual direction. People went, even though they had no grave sins, and they went more frequently. It is the practice we have today, although many more people took advantage of the sacrament two or three generations ago than they do now. I think a person should go as often as they find it helpful, at least once or twice a year just to help themselves grow spiritually.

The sacrament of reconciliation is one of the most rewarding parts of being a priest, especially when I know I have helped lift a burden of guilt and self-hatred off a person's conscience. I am blest to be able to participate in the process of bringing God's love and peace to someone. I might mention that we have our penance service this Wednesday. There is an insert in today's bulletin describing how to make a good confession. Amen.

Palm Sunday of the Passion of the Lord
March 24, 2013

HOMILY – (Isaiah 50:4-7; Philippians 2:6-11; Luke 22:14-23:56) I first want to say thank you for your prayers and good wishes for my operation. It's been four weeks since my knee was replaced and I am being told it is progressing quite well; however, I sure am tired. I am trying to conserve as much energy as possible because it's going to be a busy week. So I hope you will forgive me for being brief today.

When I was a child in grade school I often suffered with asthma, and I found that meditation on the sufferings of Jesus was a tremendous source of comfort and strength for me. If what I have to say this afternoon does not offer much to inspire you, there is a great deal of scripture we've just heard that might offer some other ideas for your reflection. The main part of today's gospel that strikes me is the question that comes up in the central part of Jesus' trial. Who is this Jesus who suffered, died and rose from the dead? He entered Jerusalem with exciting shouts from a crowd of followers: "Blessed is the king who comes in the name of the Lord." He was arrested for the same reason for which he was praised: that he was the Christ, the messiah, the Jewish savior and king. When he was accused of being a king, he could have said he wasn't who they said he was - and the trial would have been over. He would have been set free, for there was little else they could accuse him of. But when asked if he were the Messiah, the Christ, he would not deny that that's who he was: "you say that I am!" he answered the chief priests and the governor, Pontius Pilate.

His ambiguous answer as to who he was seems to challenge us: do we just call him our king; do we come to him crying "hosanna" which means "save us" when we want something. Would we be hesitant to stand up for him as our king in spite of a noisy crowd who call for his crucifixion. Who is this Jesus we honor today? It is faith in the resurrection that ultimately gives us the answer to this question.

Holy Thursday
March 28, 2013

HOMILY – (Exodus 12:1-8, 11-14; 1 Corithians 11: 23-26; John 13:1-15) A little five year-old child and his mother were on their way to McDonald's one evening, and on the way they passed a car accident. The mother and her son would usually say a prayer for whoever might be hurt whenever they passed by an accident or saw an ambulance. The mother pointed the accident out to her son and said we should say a prayer. So her son fervently offered his prayer: "dear God, please don't let those cars block the entrance to McDonald's." *Reader's Digest, Laughter the Best Medicine*, pg 89.

Eating, it's an important priority in most people's lives, isn't it? We don't like anything to get in the way when we're ready to eat. For almost all of us, eating has become more than just a way to stay alive. It is often a way to celebrate, a way to enjoy good friends, a way to remember important occasions such as a birthday, an anniversary, a holy day or holiday. God made the eating of a special meal a way for the Jews to remember that he led them to freedom, made them his chosen people and expected them to live lives of holiness as his chosen people. Without special ways to remember, we can easily forget and so in our first reading we hear the story of how the Passover came about.

It was this celebration of remembrance of having been chosen by God as his special people that Jesus and his disciples were commemorating at the Last Supper. At the supper Jesus surprised his apostles by revealing a new way in which God was about to extend his saving love to all people. With bread he gave them to eat he said: "this is my body that is for you. Do this in remembrance of me." And with a cup of wine he gave them to share he said: "This cup is the new covenant in my blood. Do this, as often as you drink it in remembrance of me." What a shock that must have been to their sensibilities - those who grew up having to drain every drop of blood out of the food they ate, now being told to take this cup of Jesus' blood and drink it, and through it they would have entered into a covenant, a commitment of love with him. Our second reading, which describes this event, is a very important one because it is the earliest description of the Eucharist that we have, written 15 years before the first gospel was written.

This is one of the most difficult parts of our faith for many people today. In the scientific culture in which we live, we look for proof and evidence. We have an attitude of "seeing is believing;" the gospels see things the other way: "believing is seeing." Until we believe, we will not see this mystery. That's basically what Jesus told Peter: "unless I wash you, you will have no inheritance with me." Before Jesus can fill us with his love, we must surrender ourselves to him in faith.

In our gospel we see there is one more thing Jesus asks of us, he asks for our faith and he also asks for our love, our love for him and for one another. I have washed your feet; you ought to wash one another's feet. "I have given you a model to follow, so that as I have done for you, you should also do." He who came to serve and not to be served asks us to serve one another in love.

St. Thomas Aquinas teaches us a lesson on food that applies to the Eucharist and pulls all these ideas together. I will end with this. Thomas says when we eat something, it is turned into who we are. That bowl of spaghetti we had for supper last evening has now become our human flesh and muscle, brain and bone. It has become us. When we receive Christ in the Eucharist, however, we do not turn him into ourselves, but we become him; we are raised up to share in his nature, to be more like him. The more we are fed on him, the more we become like him. Amen.

Good Friday
March 25, 2005

HOMILY – (Isaiah 52:13–53:12, Hebrews 4:14-16; 5:7-9, John 18:1–19:42) He was born and grew up in an obscure village, the child of ordinary people. He worked as a carpenter and an itinerant preacher. He never wrote a book, never held an office, never had a wife or children, nor owned a house. He never traveled two hundred miles from the place where he was born. When he was only thirty-three his enemies had him nailed to a cross. His executioners gambled for his clothing. He was laid in a borrowed grave. After nineteen centuries he is the central figure of the human race. All the kings that ever reigned, all the armies that ever marched have not affected the human race as much as that one solitary life.

So many times I am asked why Christ died as he did? For one thing, everything would be different. I'm sure when many of us have read history we've asked ourselves what would things be like if a certain event hadn't happened. What if Columbus had not been so determined to sail to the West Indies? Or what if the British had crushed the revolution of their thirteen colonies here in the new world in the late 1700's? Or what if the South had won the Civil War in 1864? Or what if Mr. and Mrs. Edison had decided to stop having children after their sixth one? Thomas Alva Edison, who was their seventh child, would not have been born. It's interesting to speculate how our lives would have been different if one person or one event had not been. But what about Jesus? What if he hadn't died as he did? Maybe being divine he would have been taken up directly into heaven without having to die. If, like Elijah, he was carried to heaven in a fiery chariot, some obscure Jewish history book might have mentioned him, but would that gain him a great following? Or, since Jesus was also human like us in every way except sin, he may have died a natural death, which would have resulted in his soon being forgotten after all his followers died. Think about it. Do you suppose, in either case, his followers would have risked their lives to go out preaching about him or would anyone have taken the time to write down what he said or did? Would any of us have even heard about him?

Perhaps we would still be worshipping Jupiter and Mars and Venus, or sacrificing our children to Baal or Moloch. In pagan mythology, humans were not loved by the gods. Humans were only useful to the gods for the sacrifices and worship they offered. Would we have ever heard the message of God's love and mercy? Or perhaps somewhere along the line, our ancestors might have recognized the superiority of the Jewish faith over paganism and we would all be observing Jewish traditions, abstaining from pork and making sure our infant boys were circumcised. Or maybe we all would have no spiritual anchor, wondering what life is all about, wondering if there is any kind of life after we die, wondering how God or the gods want us to serve him or her or them?

I strongly suspect that if Jesus did not die as he did and rise again, at least a billion people in today's world would be thinking, praying, acting, living differently than they are now, and with many people living life differently, everyone else would be affected. When I am asked why did Jesus have to die as he did, one answer that can be given is that we probably would never have known about him if he hadn't. That's far from a complete answer to the question, though. Theologians have struggled with this question for centuries and they have come up with many different answers. So I would like to reflect on just a couple of other ways to look at the passion of Jesus.

We can't just look as his death in isolation from the rest of his life. His whole life was dedicated to teaching God's ways and assuring us of God's love. He came to tell us God has wonderful plans for us if we believe in him and follow him. His death was the culmination of a life of love. His teachings threatened the powerful people of his day. They were so threatened by him that they felt they had to kill him. However, Jesus loved his Father enough to stay with the job he had been given, to preach the truth. And he loved the people enough to keep teaching them, no matter what the consequences might be. He could have easily given up preaching, he could have gone into hiding, he could have gotten twelve legions of angels to give him security. But if he had done anything other than be faithful to his mission, he would have betrayed the unfailing and never-ending love he proclaimed.

We could talk for hours, and still not exhaust the meaning and significance of Jesus' passion. That's why we commemorate it every week, every day even! By his death he taught us how to be patient in suffering, and to hope in the face of defeat. He taught us that goodness can overcome evil and sin, and that death does not have the last word. And in his death and resurrection he gave us a new way to pray. The night before he died he gave us the greatest prayer there is – the Eucharist. It is a prayer that unites us with him in his saving death and resurrection, and it is a prayer that shows us the perfection of faithfulness and love and gives us the help to model our lives on it.

We've all bought things that we have to assemble ourselves. Someone manufactured the item, and packed it in a box and then left it to us to put together. Jesus has done everything possible to make eternal life available to us. But we have to do the job of incorporating Jesus' saving work into our own lives. We can't leave it in the box and expect it to work. We have to live it each day. Today we honor Jesus' sacrifice and love. We pray we will do what we need to do to make it a part of our lives.

Easter
March 31, 2013

HOMILY – A pastor was telling some of the little children in school about Jesus' arrest and crucifixion. As he was teaching them about some of Jesus' last words on the cross, he asked: "What was the last thing Jesus said before he died?" One little child raised his hand and answered, "Jesus said: 'I'll be back.'"

Jesus didn't quite phrase it that way, but he did say "in a little while you will not see me, and then a little while later you will see me." He also said, "it is because I am going to the Father." (Jn 16:16) Even though by now Jesus had predicted his death and resurrection three times, the Apostles had no idea what Jesus was talking about - it took the full experience of seeing Jesus arrested, condemned, crucified, and buried, and then to find the tomb empty three days later, as well as having him personally appear to them, eat with them and show them his wounds. St. Paul's Letter to the Corinthians and the various gospels tell us of a number of appearances that took place before the apostles fully started to believe.

But once they did, and once the Holy Spirit came

down on them, they were a force that could not be stopped in spreading the "good news" that Jesus had risen.

They had seen Jesus raise dead people back to life, namely, the daughter of Jairus, the son of the widow of Naim and Jesus' friend Lazarus who lived in Bethany. But those were temporary resurrections; those people would die again. Jesus' resurrection was totally different; he could not die again, his human body was filled with divine life, which is eternal life. His body took on the properties of a spirit, yet it was not a spirit, it was real flesh and blood.

Jesus' resurrection was the beginning of something totally new and different. It is a mystery that opens up to us eternal life. He came not just to die and rise for his own benefit, but for us, that we too might live with him forever. Jesus said, "I came that they might have life and may have it to the full." (Jn 10:10)

Today's feast is the most important feast in the whole year. If Jesus had not risen, we would never have heard of him. The apostles would never have preached about him nor would they have given their lives for what they preached. Through the resurrection and the power of the Holy Spirit, Jesus' kingdom began to grow and it continues to grow in spite of 2000 years when there was always someone who was trying to destroy it. Tonight we gather in his memory, tonight we hear again the story of his victory over death, tonight we receive the sacraments that keep us united with him and growing in his life and his love.

Tonight we give praise for all that God has done for us in Jesus and tonight I wish all of you a blessed Easter. I pray that the light of the Easter fire might burn in your hearts throughout the rest of the year. Amen.

Second Sunday of Easter
April 7, 2013

INTRODUCTION – (Acts 5:12-16; Rev. 1:9-11a, 12-13, 17-19; John 20:19-31) A new power has revealed itself in our world through the resurrection of Jesus. It is a creative power, a power that offers eternal life and peace and joy and love, a power that is not aimed at the destruction of anything, except for the destruction of sin. We see that power at work in its various forms today. In today's gospel we see that power at work on Easter Sunday night in that death could not destroy Jesus, but his resurrection was the beginning of eternal life for him and for all who followed him. Jesus shared with his followers the same Holy Spirit that filled him and he gave them the gift to be able to forgive sins by his power.

Our first reading shows how the Church grows rapidly from the beginning due to the preaching of the apostles and the gifts of healing given to the early church. When we hear our second reading, we realize this was a time many years later. The Church was going through a time of serious persecution. God assured his people he would not leave them. "Do not be afraid," he told them. He begins to reveal what the future holds for God's people, difficult times, but victory when it's all over.

HOMILY – A mother took her little three year-old son to Mass for the first time. The child got impatient waiting for Mass to start. Turning to his mother the boy asked, "When does Jesus get here?"

I wonder if that's what the Apostle Thomas was asking himself all week after the other apostles had told him they had seen the Lord. It must have been dreadful wondering if Jesus would appear again and if so when. It happens, not by accident, that Jesus appears the following Sunday; I say not by accident, because Sunday would replace the Sabbath and would become the day on which Christ's followers would meet together to hear the teachings of the apostles about Jesus.

My early days as a priest proved to be very difficult times. It was right after the second Vatican Council, and there was a lot of stress that came along with the changes of Vatican II. Going out into a career of being a street cleaner was much more appealing sometimes than teaching school and adjusting to new ways of doing things. I didn't have any problem with the changes of Vatican II but some of the pastors I lived with sure didn't like them and they didn't particularly like anyone who promoted them. I prayed for peace inside myself. One day I heard this gospel where Jesus said to his apostles: "Peace be with you." I had heard it many times before, but on that particular occasion it sounded as if Jesus was speaking to me personally: "Peace be with you!" I thought, "well, why shouldn't peace be with me. It's something Jesus wants for me and it's something I wanted for myself" so when I prayed for peace, I knew it had to come. It did, slowly but definitely. When you pray for something you know Jesus wants and you want too, how can it not happen?

There are a lot of things in today's gospel that will lead us to peace: the presence of the Holy Spirit in our lives, the forgiveness of sins, the gathering in prayer on the Lord's day and hearing his word, the act of faith we make in Jesus, even if we have not seen him with our eyes. Even in the midst of later persecutions, which the Church had to face, Jesus said, "Do not be afraid."

How can a person not have peace if peace is something we want for ourselves and it is something Jesus wants for us (and it is something only he can give)? Peace be with you. Amen.

Third Sunday of Easter
April 14, 2013

INTRODUCTION – (Acts 5:27-32, 40b-41; Rev. 5:11-14; John 21:1-19) The risen Lord continues to be the focus of all of our Scripture readings today. I would like to comment on our second reading first, the Book of Revelation. John, the author of the book, had just attempted to describe his ecstatic vision of God in heaven. In the vision God had in his hand a scroll. The scroll is a central focus of the book of Revelations for the scroll revealed the events that were to occur in the future. However, the scroll was sealed with seven seals and only the risen Christ was capable of breaking open the seals so the scroll could be read. The risen Christ is described as a lamb that had been killed, killed but who was victorious over sin and death and every form of evil. In this very short passage, every creature in heaven and earth is praising God the Father and the victorious Lamb of God, the risen Lord, who could open up the scroll. It is worth pointing out that the Lamb on the front of our altar is the symbol of the victorious and risen Christ from the Book of Revelation.

Today's first reading is taken from the Acts of the Apostles. It is shortly after the resurrection and the ascension of Jesus. The apostles Peter and John are on trial before the supreme Jewish religious body, the Sanhedrin, because they were preaching and healing in the name of Jesus. They had already received one warning to stop talking about Jesus. Freedom of speech was not part of their constitution. The trial is very interesting and has been summarized quite a bit. I think the most important part of the story is the joy the apostles experienced because they could suffer for the sake of Christ.

HOMILY – Just about every time we hear the Scriptures on Sunday, we have to adjust our mind to a different timeframe with each reading. Today is no exception. Our gospel takes place just a few weeks after the resurrection of our Lord. We are told it was only the third time that Jesus appeared to the disciples. From that appearance of Jesus to the trial of the apostles narrated in our first reading, just a few weeks had passed by, but a lot of things occurred, especially the coming of the Holy Spirit on the disciples. As a result they were super-charged with divine power and enthusiasm and they didn't waste any time going everywhere to preach about Jesus and to heal people in his name. That's how they got into trouble with the Jewish leaders and got themselves arrested. When we get to our second reading from Revelation we come to a time when the Church had grown considerably and was being persecuted. It was during this time that the Book of Revelation was written, which could have been from 64 AD when Nero started his persecutions until the end of the century.

One of the main characters who stands out in today's readings is St. Peter. We remember how Peter denied Jesus when Jesus was arrested and persecuted. In today's gospel, just a few weeks after the resurrection, Jesus gave Peter a chance to undo his cowardly denial when he asked Peter three times "Do you love me?"

We see three significant moments in Peter's life in today's readings: when Peter denied Jesus, when Peter professed his love for Jesus and when, through the power of the Spirit, Peter lost all fear and boldly spoke up before the 71 Jewish leaders in the Sanhedrin that: "We must obey God rather than men." God's grace continued to work powerfully in Peter even to his laying down his life for his Lord during the reign of Nero in 64 AD.

I want to digress for a moment right now and discuss a little theology about Peter and his position as head of the Church, so please try not to lose me. Perhaps 40 or 50 years after Peter had been martyred, John wrote his gospel. Why do you suppose John would have remembered this conversation between Jesus and Peter and would have made it a part of his gospel? Was it just because it was a nice story? It was, of course, because it showed Jesus' merciful forgiveness, but it also shows something else. Each time Jesus asked, "Do you love me?" Jesus followed it up with a mission: "feed my lambs; feed my sheep." Why make an issue of this special mission given to Peter after he had long been dead? The most obvious reason I see is that it was not a personal prerogative of Peter to be shepherd of God's people, but it emphasized a position of responsibility that Jesus was giving to Peter that was meant to endure. Peter's successors (Linus, and Anacletus and Clement I all the way to our present Pope Francis) would continue serving in the ministry that Jesus gave to Peter, to feed Christ's people.

One last idea I want to leave with you is Jesus' question to Peter, "do you love me?" This is the same question he regularly asks us. He knows we are imperfect; he knows we fail him in times of weakness, pride, greed, etc. What he wants to know is that we sincerely love him and when we do then he forgives all our failings. He does, however, ask us to share in his work of growing God's kingdom. Last Sunday is often called Divine Mercy Sunday. Some people are not very happy with me that I don't make a special homily about Divine Mercy Sunday. My view is that any time we've done wrong, God's mercy is there for us if we repent and we can sincerely say to Jesus as Peter did: "you know all things, you know that I love you." Amen.

Fourth Sunday of Easter
April 21, 2013

INTRODUCTION – (Acts 13:14, 43-52; Rev. 7:9, 14b-17; John 10:27-30) The Book of Revelation requires a lot of explanation, which we do not have time for - but at least I want to give some background so today's second reading won't be a total mystery. Last week we heard John, the author of Revelation, describe some of what he saw in his vision of heaven. God had in his hand a scroll on which it had been written what was to take place in the future. The scroll was sealed with seven seals. Only the Lamb of God, that is the Risen Jesus, was able to open the seals. That was last week's reading. John went on to tell us that as the seals were opened, war and terror came about on the earth. The Book of Revelation does not delight in horror; it was simply warning God's people what they were to prepare for and to offer hope to those who suffer, especially those who suffer for being faithful to Christ. This is where today's reading takes us. One of the 24 elders standing before God's throne interprets one of John's visions of heaven. John sees God's holy people surrounding God's throne and praising him. They are dressed in white, symbolizing their inner holiness, and they are holding palm branches as a symbol of their sharing in Christ's victory over sin and death. Their sufferings are over, God will protect them, and the Lamb of God will shepherd them and provide for all their needs.

In our first reading we join St. Paul on his first missionary journey. We are in Antioch in Pisidia, a small city in what is today the central part of Turkey. Along with Paul is his companion Barnabas. Jewish communities were scattered all throughout the Roman Empire. Paul made two visits to the local Jewish synagogue there. His first visit was so successful that when he returned the following week he filled the house. But his second visit wasn't nearly so successful as we will now hear.

HOMILY – It has been a tumultuous week, bombings in Boston, an explosion in a fertilizer plant in West Texas, letters to congressmen carrying poisonous powder, not to mention the ongoing problems in the Middle East and North Korea. When we experience things like we did this week, we wonder, where is God in all this? This question has been asked since the beginning of human history. Primitive people often felt that when bad things happened, the gods were angry with them and were punishing them for their evil ways or for their failure to honor the gods. Modern people often tend to deny that there is a God, that no God would allow these things to happen.

2500 years ago the Jewish people came up with their explanation of why evil happens. They told the story of when God created all things he saw that it was very good. God put his human creatures in a garden of paradise where they would find perfect happiness. They did have to obey one law God gave them. They chose not to obey, and their pride led them to lose the happiness God had intended for them. Even at that very time that they lost what happiness God intended for them, God promised his first human creatures that there would be redemption. God would send a person who would destroy the power of evil and crush its head.

In the fullness of time, God did send a redeemer, a redeemer who calls us to hear his voice: "my sheep hear my voice," he tells us. If we follow him he promises us eternal life and that we will never perish. The image of the Good Shepherd is an image that Jesus' listeners would immediately understand.

In a more modern way of thinking, Jesus is telling us that hearing him is where we are to get our values, the standards and principles that guide our lives and affect in a major way our happiness or unhappiness in life. If we don't let his wisdom guide us, how will we seek to find direction in life, or how will we give our children values and ideals? That is part of the problem with the world today; the values that Christ taught us are being ignored. Like our first parents, we make up our own rules to our own disadvantage because we figure we know better than God what will lead us to fulfillment and happiness. Jesus' words, however, to us are clear: "my sheep hear my voice, I know them and they follow me. I give them eternal life and they shall never perish." It would take a lifetime to answer all the problems about evil in the world. I just wanted to leave you with a few things to think about.

The garden of paradise is being offered to us again. We choose it by choosing to follow the way Christ has shown us. That doesn't mean that along the way the path will be smooth and easy. The garden of paradise is not for this world but for the next. There will always be bumps and disappointments and tears in this world. During those times we have to remember St. Paul's words: "for those who love God, all things work out for the best." That's what has always helped me to remain positive even during the most difficult times.

Today is vocation Sunday. We pray every week for vocations, but on Good Shepherd Sunday we are reminded of the important role religious vocations have in guiding us in the ways of Christ. This is the life I have been living for almost 49 years now and it has been a privilege. I've had wonderful times as a priest and difficult times too, but has anyone ever been able to escape difficult times in this life. As I look back over the years, I suspect if I had lived my life in any other way than as a priest, I would not have found the happiness I did. I just wanted to put in a good word for the religious life and I would like to see others come forward with a similar desire to serve him as a priest, deacon (permanent deacon), religious brother or sister. Please keep that in your prayers today. Amen.

Fifth Sunday of Easter
April 28, 2013

INTRODUCTION – (Acts 14:21-27; Rev. 21:1-5a; John 13:31-33a, 34-45) - Last Sunday we heard a little bit about Paul's first missionary journey. His preaching and miraculous works led many people, both Jews and Pagans, to faith in Jesus as the Messiah. At the same time there, was a considerable amount of opposition to his teachings. In today's first reading, Paul is on his return trip to Syria. In spite of the harsh treatment he had previously received from his opponents in various towns and cities, he is not afraid to revisit those places. The name "Antioch" is confusing for there were two cities named Antioch. The first was a town in central Turkey where a mob of unbelievers ran Paul out of town. The second Antioch was the third largest city in the Roman Empire. It was a city on the east coast of Syria and it was where Paul's missionary journey began. Paul was returning there to report on the successes and challenges of his mission. On his way back home, he warned his converts that living the gospel is not always easy. He told them: "It is necessary for us to undergo many hardships to enter the kingdom of God."

HOMILY – This is a true story. Archbishop Leibold, who was our bishop about 40 years ago, was at a local parish for confirmation. Some of you who are older remember the custom at that time was to confirm children in the third grade. The Archbishop used to ask the children questions before he confirmed them. That this was right after the Vatican Council when a lot of religious education programs had tossed out the catechisms and taught about nothing but love. Well Archbishop Leibold started asking questions somewhat like "what was the name of Jesus' mother?" A hand went up and the child answered. "love." "How many apostles did Jesus have?" Another hand went up and the child answered. "love." This happened two or three more times before the Archbishop decided this question and answer session was going nowhere, so he went back to the altar to continue the service. The children's teacher did a good job emphasizing love, but missed out on teaching them a few other important things.

Now love is the answer to many things, and if that's all we knew and practiced about our faith we would probably be in good standing with God as long as it is the kind of love Jesus is talking about. The only problem with "love" is that it has so many meanings. We can distort it to make it mean almost anything we want. Today Jesus tells us he is giving us a new commandment: to love one another. Hearing this we may wonder what is so new about love. It is the meaning he gives it when he tells us, "As I have loved you, so also you should love one another." "As I have loved you" are the key words here. Jesus wants us to love as he did. He loved with perfect obedience to the Father and with such total unselfishness that he gave his life totally for us. Who of us could ever live up to that high ideal? His love is out of our league. He loved with a love that was divine. How could we humans ever love with so great a love? We can, but only with his help and only with his presence in our hearts. It takes emptying our hearts of pride, selfishness, greed, lust, envy, laziness, etc. That's a big order and that's why we are here today, to remember Jesus' love for us and to let it inspire us to imitate him. He even told us to do what we are doing in his memory. We are also here to be more closely united with Jesus for he told us without me you can do nothing.

Our second reading today is one of the last chapters of the Book of Revelation. If you have ever challenged yourself to read through it, you will surely remember how it tells of all the natural and supernatural catastrophes that were to take place. But that's not the main point of Revelations. Today's second reading is leading us to the main point. It describes where our future is headed if we remain faithful to God. Revelations promises a new world where death and suffering will no longer exist, where those who have loved God and loved each other as Jesus commands of us will abide with God in eternal love and joy. Amen.

Sixth Sunday of Easter
May 5, 2013

INTRODUCTION – (Acts 15:1-2, 22-29; Revelation 21:10-14, 22-23; John 14:23-29) After the resurrection and Jesus had ascended into heaven, the Apostles and the little following who believed in Jesus were Jews. They did not see themselves as part of a new religion; thus they continued to follow their Jewish laws, customs, rituals and traditions. However, there were problems when Gentiles started to believe in Jesus. Many Jews who accepted Jesus as their savior and messiah insisted that Gentiles had to adopt Jewish ways if they wanted to consider themselves followers of Jesus. So when our first reading speaks of circumcision, it's really talking about all the rules and customs the Jews were bound to follow

- dietary laws, feast days, etc. This conflict arose especially in Antioch, in Syria, because it was a large city and racially quite diverse. To solve the problem, the leaders of the Church at Antioch, including St. Paul, went to Jerusalem to meet with some of the other Apostles. Paul insisted that we are saved by Jesus' death and resurrection and the Jewish traditions and laws, other than moral and ethical laws like the Ten Commandments, were no longer required for salvation. With support from St. Peter, Paul's views were accepted by the group. Their decision was sent back to Antioch. It was a major decision, a decision that would affect how the Church would grow. Perhaps Gentiles would never have accepted Christ as their savior if they also had to be circumcised and follow Jewish laws and traditions. Bacon and ham and pork chops would be forbidden as well as shrimp and clams and crabs. If the Apostles had decided that those who followed Christ had to live by Jewish customs and laws, that would have led to only a few Christians in the world today - probably mostly Jewish - rather than the two billion who now worship Jesus. We Gentiles might still be worshipping Zeus, Pluto, Apollo, Dionysus and Aphrodite. Notice how the Apostles introduced their decision: "It is the decision of the Holy Spirit, and ours too" That the Church is being guided by the Holy Spirit, has always been the belief of the Church whenever the bishops gather in council together with the Holy Father.

HOMILY – All throughout its history, the Church has had challenges to face. When we read about some of the challenges, like we heard about in our first reading, we wonder how the Church survived - but it did, because Christ is with his Church and it is guided by the Holy Spirit. One of the things the Apostles' decision did was to make known to the world that God's saving love reaches out to all people through Jesus Christ. I see a hint of that same idea in today's second reading from the Book of Revelation. During the Easter season this year, we hear from the Book of Revelations. The Book reminds us of the heavenly kingdom which we all hope to be part of some day. It will be a kingdom free from suffering, pain and death and there will be eternal happiness. Today's reading describes God's kingdom as a great city, known as the heavenly Jerusalem. One of the details of this description focuses on the gates into the heavenly city. Notice they face in all directions, north, south, east and west. It's a way of saying that God is inviting people from everywhere to enter. God wants to fill his house with guests. Unfortunately, in many other places in the Scriptures, we learn of those who choose not to be there.

This leads into our gospel which was taken from Jesus' words at the Last Supper according to John. Jesus had just told his apostles that soon he would reveal himself to his apostles but not to the world. One of the apostles asked what that meant. This is where our gospel begins. Jesus answered, "whoever loves me will keep my word, and my Father will love him and we will come to him and make our dwelling with him." Perhaps Jesus could have added, "we will make our dwelling with him in this life and he (or she) will make his or her dwelling with me in my Father's house in the next life."

When I was reading this passage earlier about Jesus revealing himself, I always tend to think if God or Jesus revealed himself to me, I could love him more. But in these statements of Jesus, he is telling us loving him has to precede his revealing himself to us. As Jesus said right before this gospel, "Whoever loves me will be loved by my Father and I will love him and reveal myself to him." First comes loving him, and then comes seeing him.

There is one more piece to this process. First has to come obedience. Jesus said, "whoever loves me will keep my word." In other words, love is not some nice warm fuzzy feeling, it's a practical, down to earth thing. It's more what we do than what we feel. Our culture pays attention only to the feeling part of love and that's why many people have forgotten that love involves the things we do toward God and to each other. There is the road map to the heavenly Jerusalem that Jesus is giving to us today: first is the way of obedience, which leads to love which leads to his revealing himself to us and our dwelling with him for eternity. May the Holy Spirit guide us there. Amen.

Feast of the Ascension
May 12, 2013

INTRODUCTION – (Acts 1:1-11; Ephesians 1:17-23; Luke 24:46-53) St. Luke gave us two books in the New Testament: The Acts of the Apostles and, of course, his gospel. We hear from both of them today. The gospel ends with the Ascension and the Acts of the Apostles begins with the Ascension. You'll notice when you hear the first reading from the Acts, he refers to his gospel as his "first book." It is interesting to notice that he treats the Ascension in two different ways in each of these two books. In the Acts he said the Ascension occurred 40 days after Easter, while at the end of his gospel he describes how Jesus appeared to his apostles Easter Sunday night, spoke with them, ate with them and then, on Easter Sunday night, he led them out to Bethany where he ascended into heaven. Any explanation as to why Luke described the Ascension as happening on two separate occasions is simply a guess. My own guess is that Jesus made a number of appearances to various individuals or groups during the approximately 40 days following his resurrection, but those appearances pretty much ceased after 40 days. From that time on, Jesus was present to his followers through the power of the Word as preached by the Apostles, through miracles, through the Holy Spirit, the sacraments, and the Church. St. Luke, in his second work, the Acts of the Apostles, describes Jesus' invisible presence with his followers.

HOMILY – One Mother's Day morning, two young children told their mother to stay in bed. As she lay there looking forward to being brought breakfast in bed, the smell of bacon floated up from the kitchen. Finally, the children called her to come downstairs. She found them both sitting at the table eating bacon and eggs. "As a surprise for Mother's Day," one explained, "we decided to fix our own breakfast." That's sometimes the way life goes for a mother.

Happy Mother's Day to all of the mothers who are with us today. Thank you for choosing the vocation you did and for the dedication and love you freely gave in following that vocation. I was blest with two mothers: my mother, Alice, who brought me into this world, with whom I was very close and who died when I was 14 years old. My second mother was Rosella whom my father married after Alice died. At 14 I was busy with high school activities and was testing my independence as teenagers do. Then right after high school, I was off to live at the seminary. Consequently, I didn't get quite as close to Rosella as I did with my biological mother. But I know Rosella was a loving and caring person who took good care of my younger siblings. So today I thank God for the two really good mothers I had and I thank God for the good mothers who are here today and for whom we are praying.

Besides being Mother's Day, today is also the feast of the Ascension of our Lord (a feast sometimes confused with the assumption of Mary - which is celebrated on August 15th). This feast was always celebrated 40 days after Easter, until the year 2000, when it was transferred to Sunday. The issue is not when the Ascension happened. The important thing is the lessons it teaches us. I want to mention three of these lessons.

(One) It gives us an understanding of who Jesus is. I was lately struck by the image of Jesus sitting at the right hand of the Father. We say it in the Creed every Sunday. Paul tells us also in today's second reading of Jesus seated at God's right hand. Many people here remember the days when children were taught to stand up if an adult entered the room. Even today no one in a big corporation would think of walking into their bosses' office, pull up a chair and sit down, unless they were invited to (and certainly they would not move a chair next to their boss and sit down). Certainly in the culture of Jesus, one stood in the presence of a person who was their superior. When Jesus entered the presence of his Father, he sat at his right hand, a symbol of equality with his Father. That, of course, is our theology: Jesus is God from God, light from light, true God from true God, begotten, not made, consubstantial with the Father (consubstantial means he is of the same substance, the same divine nature, as the Father). (Two) The Ascension gives us an understanding of our own destiny. God didn't put us in this world to live forever; he made us in order for us to be with him forever. Where he has gone, we hope to follow. St. Augustine says: "out of compassion for us he descended from heaven, and although he ascended alone, we also ascend, because we are in him by grace." (Reading for the feast of the Ascension.) Jesus said to his apostles at the Last Supper:

"I go to prepare a place for you and then I will come again and take you to myself, so that where I am, there you may be also." (John 14:2-3) (Three) The Ascension also gives us an understanding of our responsibilities. He said to the Apostles, "you will be my witnesses." They were, but there are many others in the world today who need to know about Jesus. Who is going to proclaim the good news of God's love to them? Dead apostles? Living people have to proclaim the good news, and it's not just up to priests and nuns. There aren't enough of us to go around. Christ's plan on getting out his message is to have his followers pass it on to others, and he didn't have a backup plan. These are three lessons today's feast teaches us: who Jesus is, what our destiny is, and that our job is witnessing to God's love. There are more but I think this is enough to think about for today.

Seventh Sunday of Easter
May 24, 1998

INTRODUCTION – (Acts 7:55-60; Rev 22:12-14, 16-17, 20; John 17:20-26) Thursday was the feast of the Ascension of Jesus into heaven. Our readings today flow from that idea. St. Stephen, the first martyr, is strengthened in his time of trial by a vision of Jesus in glory at the right hand of God the Father. The psalm refrain praises Christ who is king, the most high over all the earth. The second reading from the book of Revelation foretells the triumph of Christ our Lord over all evil and assures us that he will return again, soon. The gospel is the last part of a magnificent prayer Jesus prayed at the Last Supper. After he prayed for his disciples, he prays for all of us who would come to believe in him through their preaching his gospel.

HOMILY – Today's gospel was part of Jesus' prayer at the Last Supper. Consider the fact that he is about to die. His final prayer we would expect would express those thoughts that are deepest in his own heart. The third part of his prayer is for all of us, all who will come to believe in him and follow him. And what does he pray for us? His prayer is for unity in love. And he prays for it over and over again. He prays that as he is one with the Father, we might be one with him and one with each other.

Our culture idealizes rugged individualism, the self-made man, the guy who pulls himself up by his own boot straps, the cowboy who rides off into the sunset alone, the person who doesn't need to depend on anyone. But the reality of our lives in today's world is that we need other people in hundreds of ways. We need others for everyday necessities, for education, for employment, for inspiration, for health needs and of course we need friends and family to support us emotionally.

In our spiritual life we need to know Christ in a personal way and to have him as a friend, we need to take time for private and individual prayer, but our relationship with our Lord can't just be an individual thing only. It can't just be something between me and God to the exclusion of anyone else. If we want to be one with Christ, we're going to be one with a lot of people too. Thomas Merton said it so clearly "Without love and compassion for others, our own apparent love for Christ is fiction." Christianity is essentially a community religion. If in so many areas of our everyday lives we need others, why do we think that in our spiritual lives we can get along just fine without anyone's help? Christ has made it clear that how we reach him and how he comes to us is through others: through Scripture, through liturgy, though the faith that is passed on by being taught and lived by a community of believers, through the sacraments and through how we treat one another, especially the least of his brothers and sisters. If we say we don't need the church, we don't need other people to help us get to God, we are trying to walk to the other side of the world with only one leg. I honestly think this is the biggest sin, the biggest heresy of the modern day, because those who disassociate themselves from the Church are disconnecting themselves from the roots that provide nourishment for their faith. Without deep roots and the spiritual nourishment we need, we become an easy pushover for the devil when a moment of weakness comes.

The unity that our Lord talks about presupposes some leadership. Someone has to be in charge. If you asked a dozen people to interpret some part of scripture, or to tell you what God thinks about some issue, you would probably get a dozen different answers. Someone has to have the last word if there is going to be some unity, or people will be going in a dozen different directions. Christ was no dummy. He knew that. He had a dozen Apostles with him all the time and he knew some of the debates and discussions they got into. He gave Peter the job to be the rock, the source of stability, the focus of unity, the one to hold them all together. Again we get back to the need for the Church and the way Christ established it if we are going to be faithful to Christ, and not just be going off on our own.

Our unity with each other is not just for our own personal well-being, but it affects in a most important way the whole saving work of our Lord. Our common belief, our common set of values, our oneness in prayer and most of all in love tell the world about Jesus. Jesus said, "I pray that they may be one in us, that the world may believe that you (Father) sent me." The church's mission, which means your mission as well as mine, is not just to save ourselves, but to bring God's saving grace and life to others too. Staying united is one of the primary ways we will do it. When we all go our own individual ways, our efforts become significantly less effective.

We're all together in this world; we're all together in our spiritual journey too. Jesus wants us to live as one with him and as one with each other. This was his greatest desire for us his followers. This is one of the experiences that mystics have described. Mystics, those who are closest to God, have an innate sense of how interconnected we all are. I want to tell you the story of an old man whose experience at the Washington Vietnam Veterans Memorial was somehow a mystical experience. He was weeping noticeably as he stood at the Memorial. Moved by the sight, a young man waked over to the old man, put his hand on his shoulder and said, "Is one of these yours, sir?" The old man said softly, "Not one of them, son! All of them!"

Vigil of Pentecost
May 19, 2013

INTRODUCTION – (Genesis 11:1-9; Romans 8:22-27; John 7:37-39) There are eleven possible readings for the feast of Pentecost, six for the vigil and five for the feast itself. On Sunday there is a special sequence before the gospel. Only Easter and Pentecost have a special sequence that is required and Corpus Christi has an optional one. Today is indeed a special feast, the third most important feast in the Church year, the feast that celebrates the completion of Jesus' saving work with his sending of the Holy Spirit. Thanks to those who wore red, the color of the Holy Spirit.

Our first reading today is from Genesis. The story

follows the story of the great flood. Those who survived the flood intended to make sure they would be able to escape floods in the future, so they decided to build a high tower. Notice a little satire here. In their pride, they are going to build a tower up to the heavens and God decides to "come down" to see what's going on. He confuses their speech to put an end to their prideful building project. God does not want to divide people but to unite them. In the account of Pentecost, in a passage that is read Sunday from the Acts of the Apostles, that's exactly what he does as he gives the apostles a special gift of tongues so that people from every nation would understand the message of God's universal love that they were preaching.

HOMILY – Two hundred years ago this year, a man was born named Antoine Frederic Ozanam. He was a distinguished scholar, a journalist, a doctor of law, a doctor of letters and a professor of law as well as a professor of foreign literature at the Sorbonne in Paris. In his short life (of 40 years) as a professor, a father and a husband, he managed to found a society to help the poor, the Conference of Charity, which today is known as the society of St. Vincent de Paul. St. Vincent de Paul was a French saint who dedicated himself to helping the poor 200 years before Blessed Frederic Ozanam was born. I call Ozanam blessed because Pope John Paul declared him blessed in 1997, the last step before sainthood. Why do I tell you this? Not just because it's the 200th anniversary of his birth, but also because it is one example of the Holy Spirit at work. The Spirit inspired Frederic Ozanam, a layman, to live a life of learning, scholarship and holiness. We have a parish that generously supports a food pantry and generous volunteers who help distribute the food on Saturday afternoon. That is how the Spirit inspires a lot of people (donors and workers) to help over 100 people monthly who need help.

I have a success story I would like to tell you from our St. Vincent de Paul work. There was a man named Rodney who came in for food. He was an ex-con who had put in his time. One time when he came in he asked Kathleen, who works in the food pantry, for a skillet. When she was shopping later in the week, she bought one and gave it to him. This fired up his interest in cooking. He joined a cooking class at the Freestore and in a short time he became such a good cook that he is now the kitchen manager at the Freestore and works there also as liaison between P & G and the Freestore. His story has inspired some of his buddies who were down and out to realize they too could improve their lot in life. I see this story also as the work of the Spirit inspiring Kathleen to go out and get a $9.00 skillet for one of the people who came to our pantry.

Jesus spoke many times about the Holy Spirit. One thing he said that always struck me as strange is when he said, "it is better for you that I go, for if I do not go the Holy Spirit will not come to you." (Jn 16:7) Surely the apostles wondered, as I did, how could anything be an advantage, how could anything be better for them if Jesus were to leave them. As we now know, Jesus didn't really leave them, rather he remained with them through the Holy Spirit he sent them. Here is one of the advantages of having the Holy Spirit. Jesus physically could not be everywhere, but through the Spirit, Jesus could be touching the hearts and minds of all seven billion people in the world today, if they were all receptive to his Spirit.

It is hard to imagine the Holy Spirit for the Holy Spirit chooses to stay out of the spotlight and prefers to work behind the scenes. The Spirit is with us now when we come together in faith and prayer. The Spirit helps us to listen to God's word. We pray for the Spirit to change bread and wine into Christ's body and blood. The Spirit guides the Church, and the Church still survives even when the Church leaders and members do not always let themselves be guided by the Spirit. The Spirit blesses our inner spirits with love, joy, peace, patience, kindness, goodness, faithfulness, humility and self-control, gifts that Paul lists in Galatians (5:22 & 23). With all that the Spirit does, what does the Spirit not do? The Spirit does not force us. God gave us a free will and the Spirit does not take that away. The Spirit inspires us to move in God's direction, but it's our choice whether or not we do so. The Spirit guides and inspires the whole Church and the Spirit guides and inspires each one of us individually. In (Sunday's) gospel we hear Jesus say the Spirit "will teach you everything and remind you of all that I told you." That is one of the ways I have experienced the Spirit working in my life, reminding me what I should do, how I should live, and helping the Scriptures come alive for me. Sometimes in counseling I have experienced an idea coming into my head that was just the right thing to say to a person and I end up asking myself, "where did that idea come from?" For a long time all I ever knew of the Spirit was he would help us when we had to take a test. Here too the Spirit helps, but the Spirit also teaches us to be responsible, and I've found if I didn't do my homework, the Spirit wasn't going to whisper the answers in my ears. If we had another hour, I couldn't say everything that could be said about the Spirit. Just open you own heart to the Spirit and discover the blessings the Spirit can bring. Jesus promised the Father would send the Spirit to those who ask him for the Holy Spirit. (Lk. 11:14)

Feast of the Holy Trinity
May 26, 2013

INTRODUCTION – (Prov. 8:22-31; Romans 5:1-5; John 16:12-15) There are a number of books in the Old Testament called wisdom books. The books discuss topics such as the meaning of life or the meaning of suffering as well as practical ideas on how to raise children or how to handle your money. Sometimes wisdom is pictured as a person; for example, wisdom is often pictured as a woman who tirelessly tries to lead people away from foolishness and sin. In today's reading from Proverbs, wisdom is described as a person who was with God before creation and who helped God create the world. This is not to be understood as a reference to the Trinity. It was Christ who revealed the mystery of the Trinity and the Book of Proverbs was composed about 500 years before Christ. With our present theology of the Trinity, however, we can see a vague foreshadowing of what was to be revealed at a later time in the teachings of Jesus.

HOMILY – I'm sure most people here have read a mystery novel or watched a movie about a murder mystery. As the story moves on, we keep getting information about the characters and we get clues that encourage us to try to figure out the mystery. Usually a good mystery, if it's well done, never allows us to figure out the ending until the end – then it all fits together and makes sense.

We are faced with several mysteries as a part of our faith. We are given various pieces of information about the mystery, but it doesn't all fit together yet. Someday it will when we know God more fully and completely, but we're still working on that.

The one piece of information we have about God is that there is only one God. In a culture where people worshipped multiple gods, sometimes in the hundreds, God insisted on the Jews undivided loyalty. In those days, people believed that gods were local. For example, if you lived in Egypt, the Egyptian gods held power. If you lived in Babylon, the Babylonian gods held power. But for Israel, no matter where they traveled, their God was the God over all gods. God's covenant with them was "I am the Lord thy God, thou shalt not have strange God's before me." Before the Babylonian exile (in 587 B.C.), the Jews may have believed that some of the other gods of other nations were real, even if not as powerful as their God. Eventually, the Jews became convinced that all the other gods were just a piece of wood or stone or metal and were nothing at all. It was a hard lesson for the Jews to learn, but they finally caught on after the Babylonian exile.

The next piece of information we have about God is what Jesus revealed to us. He showed he had amazing power, he was an outstanding teacher, he had power over evil, he showed infinite love, he had authority to forgive sins and give an authoritative interpretation of God's law, and he had this special relationship with God whom he called Father. All these things showed he was someone more than human. However, when he rose from the dead, ascended to heaven and was seated at the right hand of the Father, his followers recognized him as God and worshipped him as God. It was difficult for the early believers to understand how God could be one, yet they could not deny their experience of Jesus as Son of the Most High, the Son of God, the Savior whose kingdom would last forever as the Angel Gabriel announced to Mary, his mother. Moreover, the letters of Paul and the gospel of John spoke of a third divine personality who regularly descended upon the believers and brought to them marvelous spiritual gifts.

Although the letters of Paul and the gospels were written in the first century and a simple creed, which we know as the Apostles Creed, took shape in those early years, it took many years of debate, anguish and even bloodshed before Christ's followers were able to formally and officially define their faith in this mystery of the Trinity. The term "trinity" came about in the early 200's, a word coined by Tertullian, but the final definition of our faith came about at the Council on Nicea in 325 and at the Council of Constantinople in 381. The profession of faith that came out of these two councils is prayed every Sunday in the Creed.

So there you have the mystery of the Trinity. The Father is God, the Son is God, the Holy Spirit is God. Yet, there is only one God. If I tried to explain it to you, like some theologians have tried, you would walk out of here not knowing any more than when you came in. That's not because you would not be smart enough, it's because I would be incapable of explaining it. So, today I'll spare you any attempt to explain the Trinity. Maybe next year I may attempt to explain it somewhat. If it's so profound, I have been asked, why does God want us to know anything about it at all? I'm sure it's for the same reason any lover reveals himself or herself to the person they love. God wants us to know him, to love him and to serve him. Our knowledge of the Trinity allows us to know him just a little better, even if we don't fully understand him yet. Some day we shall see God as God is, St. Paul tells us. We shouldn't be surprised that we don't fully understand God, because there are many things in this universe that we are still discovering. It stands to reason then that the creator of all that is, the Ultimate Reality, is the greatest mystery of all. Amen.

The Body and Blood of Christ
June 2, 2013

INTRODUCTION – (Genesis, 14:18-20; 1 Corinthians 11:23-26; Luke 9:11b-17) Today's first reading takes us to the Holy Land to the time of Abraham, about 1850 years before Christ. Abraham's nephew, Lot, had been captured by some local tribes and Abraham set out to rescue him, which he did. On his return, he passed by Salem, which is Jerusalem today. He was met by Melchizedek, who was both king and high priest in that district. It was not unusual at that time for the same person to be both king and high priest. Melchizedek offered bread and wine. It is hard to know whether it was offered as refreshment to Abraham or if it was offered as a sacrifice to God Most High. At any event, some of the early fathers in the Church saw this gesture as a foreshadowing of the Eucharist. (Our stained-glass window on the side depicts this scene.)

The second reading from St. Paul is especially significant in that the Letter to the Corinthians was written 10 to 15 years before the earliest gospel; thus our second reading is the oldest description of the Eucharist that is in existence today. The language Paul uses indicates this is a tradition that is authentic and reliable. He received it from the Lord and he handed it on to the Corinthians as he had received it. Receiving it "from the Lord" does not necessarily mean that he received it directly, but that it is an essential part of the gospel and has its origin in the teaching and the life of Jesus Christ.

HOMILY – To understand this first little story you have to know that here at St. Boniface on Sundays I let the Communion ministers clean the chalices back in the sacrarium. This story is about a little boy of three who was brought to Mass for the first time. He was intrigued by everything the priest was doing. At his parish after communion, the priest cleaned the chalices at the altar. When the priest finished cleaning the chalices the child turned to his mother and said: "he's finished doing dishes mom, now can we go home?"

A teenager's mother reported that when her son came home from church camp, he said: "Communion was the only decent meal they had." At that camp, there must have been a cook who couldn't cook; but on a more spiritual level the boy is right, receiving Christ in the Eucharist is infinitely superior to any other food we might be able to imagine. Jesus said, "do not labor for food that perishes, but for the food that endures for eternal life, which the Son of Man will give you." (Jn. 6:27)

Numerous times Jesus talks about faith. For example he says: "have faith," "your faith has saved you," "if you had faith the size of a mustard seed," "oh you of little faith." Today we celebrate a feast that is a great challenge to our faith: that at Mass bread and wine are changed from being bread and wine into being the body and blood of Jesus. It's not merely a symbolic reminder of Jesus; it is Jesus. His words are clear: "this is my body," "this is the cup of my blood." "Do this in memory of me."

I do not understand how people can easily accept that the Son of God became human but have difficulty accepting that the Son of God could become food and drink for us. "My flesh is real food, by blood is true drink," he tells us in John's gospel (Jn. 6:55). Unfortunately, many prefer to believe what they see rather than what Jesus tells us. When they see the host is no different after the consecration, they do not believe it is different.

How can we approach this mystery? First of all, we all know we can't always believe what we see. One proof of that is when a magician does a magic trick. We know when we are watching magic, the magician is fooling our eyes and we marvel how the magician makes it look so real. Other proof that we can't always believe what we see is that some things look very much alike and we can mistake one thing for another, such as a vitamin pill, a sleeping pill and a little piece of candy like an M & M. That's why we have to be careful where we keep our pills if there are little children around.

How can it happen that at Mass the bread and wine become Christ's body and blood? On one level, the spiritual, believing part of me says it's simply because Jesus said so. Whenever Jesus said something, it happened. So I just accept what Jesus says as it is Jesus who tells us: "have faith in me." I still try to understand this mystery from a natural perspective. One thing that helps me understand the Eucharist a little better is to think of a seed. Whether it is a microscopic seed or an avocado seed, a seed has power; it has the energy to produce life. A tiny seed can produce a giant oak tree or a huge elephant. Where does it get that energy? Ultimately God put it there. If God can put life energy in a tiny seed, God can put himself into a tiny piece of bread and transform it into his own divine self. Theologians call this transubstantiation (a change of substance). When I think this way, it helps the logical part of my mind accept the mystery a little more easily. As Jesus promises through faith in him and his divine presence in Communion, he is giving us eternal life.

How do we get that kind of faith? I think it's by constantly reminding ourselves what Jesus said when we receive Communion: "this is my body," "this is the cup of my blood," and by receiving him with that devotion and conviction. When we attend Mass and receive communion each week, our faith grows stronger; when we stay away, our faith gets weaker. Besides receiving

Jesus with faith, I would like to add we also have two holy hours each week, which are meant to help us strengthen our devotion to the Eucharist.

One more story: A mother did her best to explain the Mass to her young daughter. When she went to receive Communion and then returned to her pew the little girl asked, "When will it be my turn to have lunch with God?" A very perceptive little girl. Not only do we have lunch with God, but God provides the food: his own body and blood. Amen.

10th Sunday in Ordinary Time
June 9, 2013

INTRODUCTION – (1 Kings 17:17-24; Galatians 1:11-19; Luke 7:11-17) Eight hundred sixty years before Christ, in the northern Kingdom of Israel, there ruled a king named Ahab and a queen who was the infamous Jezebel. They promoted paganism and tried to destroy the Jewish religion. Thus they came into conflict with Elijah – one of the greatest prophets in the Old Testament. As a punishment for people turning away from God, Elijah decreed that there would be a drought and a famine over the entire Middle East and there was. To escape the wrath of Ahab and Jezebel, Elijah fled Israel to what is today southern Lebanon near Tyre and Sidon. God guided Elijah to the home of a widow. God gave her, through Elijah, a miraculous abundance of food and she in turn fed him and gave him a place to stay. While there, her only son got sick and died, and this is where our first reading begins today. It tells us that Elijah brought him back to life. This account of Elijah bringing him back to life is contrasted with the ease by which Jesus brings a person back to life with a simple command.

HOMILY – There was a wealthy man who decided he wasn't wealthy enough. So he called on help from the devil to obtain a newspaper for him that would give him all the news and stock quotes on a specific day one month in the future. He said to himself, "I'll be the richest man in the world with that information." Within a day or two a messenger came to his door with a newspaper dated one month ahead. Quickly turning to the business section, he was ecstatic for there before his eyes were the stock prices of all stocks one month in advance. But as he picked up the phone to start buying and selling stocks, he saw the obituary column and discovered his name was there. No matter what we have in life, without life we have nothing. Revelation (14:13) tells us the only thing we take with us are the works that we did – hopefully lots of good ones.

Jesus was moved with pity when he saw the man being carried out of the town to be buried. His pity was not so much for the man, but for his mother. In that culture, a widow was supported and cared for by her son, and this was her only son. It was equivalent to her losing all her "social security." She would have had no means of support, nothing. Because he pitied her, he restored the son to his mother.

Just to be accurate in our terminology, this was not a resurrection but a resuscitation. The resurrection will be forever. A resuscitation is temporary for perhaps many more years or perhaps for just a few more years. It is something that happens frequently these days when doctors or emergency workers bring a person back to life whose heart had stopped and they were clinically dead. A number of those people who are resuscitated have what are called "near death experiences." Most of the people who had near death experiences, saw a light they felt drawn to; sometimes they saw and talked with relatives, most (but not all) experienced a sense of peace. Reading about it some years ago greatly reinforced my belief in the next life. Those who had those experiences were left with three attitudes that pretty much stayed with them: 1) they no longer feared death, 2) they put less value on material things and 3) they appreciated and valued their loved ones a great deal more.

It would have been extremely interesting to interview the young man whom Jesus resuscitated in today's gospel to hear about his experiences on the other side. Notice Jesus didn't have to do anything special to resuscitate him except to speak the words: "I say to you, arise." The power of his word that healed the sick, calmed the sea, cast out demons also could raise the dead.

I might mention that last week we celebrated the feast of the Body and Blood of Christ. Because the powerful word of Jesus that could even raise the dead also said: "this is my body, this is my blood, do this in memory of me," we believe bread and wine become Christ's body and blood.

In John 10:10 Jesus tells us: "I came that they may have life and may have it to the full." I can hardly pass up this opportunity where the gift of life is a central theme of our readings and not say something about the trial against Dr. Kermit Gosnell less than a month ago in Philadelphia. The horrible things that went on in his abortion clinic just point out the grisly and immoral business of abortion. What he did to babies already born is so horrible in people's minds, but somehow when the same things are done to babies not yet born, it's not all that bad in the view of some people. It's hard for me to understand that so many people do not see that there is no essential difference between a baby not yet born and one that has been born. I'm grateful that God gave me life and my parents supported it and nurtured it. Amen.

11th Sunday in Ordinary Time
June 16, 2013

INTRODUCTION – (2 Samuel 12:7-10, 13; Galatians 2:16, 19-21; Luke 7:36-8:3) King David was a great king and loved God but, like all of us, he was not perfect. Today's reading occurs shortly after he gave in to his lust for Bathsheba and got her pregnant. Then he arranged for her husband, Uriah, to be killed in battle so he could marry her and cover up his sin. Nathan, God's prophet at the time, was given the mission of confronting the king, and that's where our reading begins. The word "Lord" as used in today's reading refers to God mostly, but "lord" also refers to David's predecessor, King Saul, as when God tells David that God had given him his lord's house and his lord's wives. The theme is on forgiveness, which corresponds to the theme in the gospel.

HOMILY – Happy Fathers' Day to all of our fathers and grandfathers. You deserve our respect and appreciation for the care and love and sacrifice you made for your families. It was hard to find a couple of jokes for fathers' day, so I've substituted a joke about a husband (I figured that was close enough). A pastor met a woman at whose wedding he had officiated years ago. "Does your husband live up to the promises he made to you before you were married?" he asked the woman. "He sure does," she immediately answered. "While we were dating he kept saying he wasn't good enough for me, and he has been proving it ever since." (*Joyful Noiseletter*, June-July 2011 and June-July 2010) That doesn't apply to any of the men here though. You are all wonderful people.

I could talk for several hours on today's theme of forgiveness because there are so many kinds of forgiveness. I could talk about the forgiveness we need to have in our dealings with one another, or I could talk about having to forgive ourselves. I've known people who couldn't forgive God because they thought God had let them down. Today, however we are going to talk about God's forgiveness of us because that is the theme of today's readings. God is always ready to forgive us when we repent, but we do have to repent. In today's first reading we heard David say to the prophet, "I have sinned against the Lord." He didn't blame someone else for what he did. He admitted his responsibility. The first step in repenting is honesty with God and with ourselves. Our psalm that follows the first reading is attributed to King David who prayed: "to you I have acknowledged my sin; my guilt I did not hide. I said, 'I will confess my transgression to the Lord' and you have forgiven the guilt of my sin." – A good expression of repentance.

I would like to turn now to our gospel. A woman with a bad reputation broke into a formal dinner and showed Jesus an overwhelming amount of gratitude and affection. A Pharisee who had invited Jesus, whose name was Simon, along with the other guests, was shocked. So Jesus told a parable about two debtors. The parable made the point that the woman's many sins had been forgiven and that was why she was so lavish in her giving thanks to Jesus, for she had been forgiven so much.

We are not told when she might have been forgiven. I would just be speculating to suggest that she may have heard Jesus preach about the mercy of God – in the parable of the lost sheep or the prodigal son, for example. Hearing his teaching on God's mercy, she may have had a conversion turning her heart to God totally. Somehow, however it came about, she knew Jesus was the agent through which she was forgiven, and she came to show her immense gratitude. (By the way, this scene is pictured in the stained glass window above the side door on the Pitt Street side of the Church.) When Jesus told her: "Your sins are forgiven," he was giving her concrete assurance that she had really been forgiven.

Time and again in the gospels Jesus said to people, "Your sins are forgiven." Jesus continues to say this to us through the sacrament of reconciliation. Theologians have always taught that it is possible to be forgiven of really serious sin by making a perfect act of contrition. But mostly serious sin is forgiven through the sacraments of baptism, reconciliation and the anointing of the sick.

Even if a person is forgiven by a perfect act of sorrow, the Church does require of Catholics a firm resolution to go to sacramental confession as soon as possible. (*Catholic Catechism* # 1452) Why does it have this requirement – because the Church knows our perfect act of contrition may not be as perfect as we think it is. Most of us are pretty good at rationalizing and confession helps us to develop an objective and honest view of our spiritual lives.

Confession can be helpful to our spiritual growth for all of us even when we don't have anything big to confess, but it is necessary for serious sins. Theology can get kind of heavy, and I can see some people's eyes starting to glaze over, so I will conclude with this: if you do not remember everything that I said today, or if you are confused because some points need a fuller explanation, I ask you to remember the two important attitudes that are expressed in today's two readings: 1) be honest with yourself like David in the first reading and 2) be thankful for God's mercy and forgiveness like the woman in the gospel. Amen.

12th Sunday in Ordinary Time
June 23, 2013

INTRODUCTION – (Zechariah 12:10-11, 13:1; Galatians 3:26-29; Luke 9:18-24) "Christ" was not Jesus' second name. The word Christ, or Christos in Greek, means the "Anointed One." In Hebrew the word for the "Anointed One" is Messiah. The Jewish view was that the Christ would be a powerful and gifted king or a cosmic judge of the earth or a great high priest who would authentically teach God's word. As God's Anointed One, the Christ would free God's people from the control of the Romans who ruled over them through a Roman Governor (at the time of Jesus it was Pontius Pilate), whose soldiers occupied their land and to whom the Jews paid taxes. In today's gospel Peter acknowledges Jesus was the Christ of God, the one they expected to free them from Roman domination. But when Jesus predicted he would suffer, be rejected and be put to death, it was as if Jesus was speaking in Chinese. It was totally beyond the apostles' ability to comprehend. We know from Jewish history that there were many good and holy people who suffered and were put to death such as the prophets or Jewish martyrs. However, in the Jewish mentality, and in all of Jewish literature, there was never even a hint that the Christ, the Messiah, would suffer or would be put to death. The Christ or the Messiah was expected to be a glorious liberator from the Romans and he would punish the Romans for their treatment of the Jews. Today's first reading from Zechariah foretells a time when God would purify his people and his people would deeply repent over one of God's servants whom they had killed. Jerusalem's mourning and repentance would lead to their purification. The person Zechariah was speaking of has never been identified, but after the resurrection, Jesus' followers could discover a new way to understand certain Old Testament scripture passages, such as today's. They found another meaning in passages about suffering and they could see how those passages applied to and were fulfilled in Jesus. St. John's gospel specifically applies today's first reading to Jesus' being pierced by a lance as he hung on the cross. "They shall look on him whom they have pierced." (Jn 19:37).

HOMILY – I want you to see today's gospel in the context of the events that precedes it. You may already know that historically all the events (miracles and teachings) in Jesus' ministry did not happen in the exact order in which they are written. Each gospel writer structured the events that were part of Jesus' ministry in a way that suited their own purpose. One simple example is the prayer "Our Father." In Matthew we find it at the beginning of Jesus' ministry in the Sermon on the Mount. In Luke, we find it more toward the end of his ministry as he is making his way to Jerusalem and the apostles ask him to teach them how to pray.

I want to speak about the context of today's gospel so you can get a better sense of the ups and downs the apostles experienced day by day in following Jesus. We're not the only ones who have ups and down in our spiritual lives. You might try to imagine you were one of the apostles and imagine experiencing what they were going through. It is in chapter nine where we find today's gospel, and chapter nine begins with Jesus sending the apostles to nearby villages to cast out demons and to heal the sick, which they discovered they had the power to do because Jesus gave it to them. Then there is a piece about Herod asking the question about Jesus, "who is this about whom I hear such things?" It might make you a little nervous to have your governor or ruler start asking questions about you: "who is that guy or that woman that I'm hearing about?" (Get the FBI to check them out!) Herod's question leads into today's gospel when Jesus asks "who do people say that I am?" Immediately before Luke's gospel today, a large crowd of about 5000 men (not counting women and children) came to Jesus to hear him speak and to be healed. While they were with him, he fed them miraculously with five loaves and two fish. These are some of the exciting things that had been happening. Then, the apostles get blown away. Typical of Luke, we are told Jesus had been in prayer before he asked the apostles two important questions: who do people say I am, and most important: who do you say that I am? Peter had the answer, but Jesus told them not to tell anyone. Why? Because Peter only had part of the answer. Jesus added the part of the answer that was missing: that he would suffer, be rejected by the authorities and be killed and on the third day be raised. As I said in my introduction, there was never any hint that the long awaited savior of Israel would suffer in any way. If we had been there, we would have been as shocked as all the apostles. But wait, that's not all. Jesus warns of sufferings for those who follow him, and maybe even death. Apparently the apostles put out of their minds everything Jesus said about suffering. They were in a state of denial and expected Jesus would do those wonderful things for God's people that they always believed he would do: get rid of the Romans and restore the Kingdom of David, which was also for them the Kingdom of God, to Israel.

In hindsight, through faith in the resurrection, we now know that Jesus, our savior and Messiah will do great and wonderful things for his people, more wonderful things than we can even imagine. It was believed in the early years of the Church that after Jesus' Ascension, he would return in glory in a very short time to establish God's kingdom. When Luke was writing his gospel, however, in around the year 85 (at least 50 years after Jesus had ascended to the Father), many of Jesus' followers became discouraged and were losing faith; they were getting tired of waiting for Jesus to return. Perhaps that's why Luke's gospel tells us to take up our cross daily – for Luke suspected it would be a long wait. Who knew we would still be waiting 2000 years later? If we have faith in Jesus, however, we still wait for his glorious return and for the fullness and joy of God's eternal kingdom. The day of the Lord will come and those who have remained faithful will share in his glory, but because it probably won't happen tomorrow and probably not even next week, we are to take up our cross daily (day by day) and follow him. Amen.

Birth of John the Baptist
June 24, 2012

INTRODUCTION – (Is 49:1-6; Acts 13:22-26; Luke 1:57-66, 80) We are familiar with John the Baptist from the readings during Advent. John was the prophet who immediately preceded Jesus and foretold his coming. John's birthday usually falls on a weekday, but it is considered such an important feast that when it falls on Sunday, it takes precedence over the Sunday readings. If you are curious why the feast of his birth is today, consider this. The feast of the Annunciation is celebrated on March 25. When the archangel Gabriel appeared to Mary, the archangel told her that her cousin Elizabeth was already in her sixth month. So add three months to March 25 and we are at June 25. (Since John's birthday is the 24th – he must have come a day early).

The liturgy usually puts the feast day of saints on the

day they died and entered into eternal life. But there are only three birthdays. This is because their birth is considered especially holy since they were born free from any sin.

[eve] – Our first reading is from Jeremiah, a prophet who lived 600 years before Christ. As God was telling Jeremiah he was to be a prophet, the reading describes that role. This description of a prophet fits John the Baptist as well.

The gospel is the annunciation to John's father, the old priest Zechariah, that he and his elderly wife would have a child, a special child who would prepare God's people for the coming of the Messiah.

[morning] – In today's first reading, the prophet Second Isaiah, who lived about 500 years before Christ, speaks of some mysterious person who was identified simply as God's servant. This poem and three others in Isaiah's writings are known as Servant Songs. The early Church found these songs described Jesus in a most uncanny way. They are usually read during Holy Week. Today, however, the liturgy applies this second of the Servant Songs to John the Baptist because it states: "the Lord called me from birth, from my mother's womb he gave me my name."

When the archangel Gabriel had appeared to John's father Zachariah nine months earlier, he told him his wife Elizabeth would have a son and he was to be named John. Zachariah and Elizabeth were a very old couple and Zachariah didn't believe the angel. Not smart! He lost the ability to speak because of his lack of faith. (It's like the angel was telling him, "keep your mouth shut and your lack of faith to yourself.") Once Zachariah gave his child the name he had been told to name him, he showed he fully accepted all that the angel told him and his ability to speak returned.

HOMILY – Since I gave a long introduction, I do not have a very long sermon. One of Aesop's most famous fables is the story of the ant and the grasshopper.

The story goes like this: In a field one summer's day, a Grasshopper was hopping about, chirping and singing to its heart's content. An Ant passed by, bearing along with great toil a kernel of corn he was taking to the nest. "Why not come and chat with me," said the Grasshopper, "instead of toiling and moiling in that way?" "I am helping to lay up food for the winter," said the Ant, "and recommend you to do the same." "Why bother about winter?" said the Grasshopper; we have got plenty of food at present." The Ant went on its way and continued its toil. When the winter came, the Grasshopper had no food and found itself dying of hunger, while it saw the ants distributing corn and grain from the stores they had collected in the summer. Then the Grasshopper knew: "It is best to prepare for the days of necessity."

Even 2500 years ago, people knew the importance of preparing for the future. It's still just as true today. If we do not learn this lesson when life is good, we'll learn the hard way when it's too late. This goes for education, investing, health and all kinds of important areas of life. John the Baptist's role in life was to insist on the need to prepare. He called people to repent and prepare for the coming of God's kingdom. His message is as important today as it ever was. There is a kind of new age theology that follows the attitude of the Grasshopper. It says don't worry. Everybody is going to be in heaven in the end (except for someone like Hitler). Although God wants all people to be saved, there are abundant passages in the Scriptures that warn us that we cannot take salvation for granted. Jesus, who came to save us and who revealed to us so clearly the love of God, warned us: "The door to heaven is narrow. Work hard to get in, because many will try to enter and will not be able." (Luke 13:23) Jesus' message at the beginning of his ministry was the same message as John the Baptist: "repent and believe in the gospel." The word "believe" means more than saying, "I believe." It means putting our belief into action. Statistics keep coming out that fewer and fewer people are coming to Church, which is an indication that more and more people believe that worship of God is not all that important. I think it's the entitlement mentality. We feel entitled to be happy (even eternally), no matter what we do or how we live. That's not what the Scriptures tell us. I think the most important lesson we can learn from this feast of John the Baptist is to prepare. The fact you are here today is one good sign that you understand we need to prepare to meet our God. Amen.

13th Sunday in Ordinary Time
June 30, 2013

INTRODUCTION – (1 Kings 19:16b,19-21; Galatians 5:1, 13-18; Luke 9:51-62) Today's gospel reading brings us to a critical point in St. Luke's gospel. St. Luke tells us at this point in his gospel that Jesus turned his face toward Jerusalem. From this point on, Luke wrote that everything Jesus said or did took place while he was on his way to Jerusalem. This part of Luke's gospel is referred to as the "journey narrative." When Jesus decided to go to Jerusalem, he knew what was ahead for him; nonetheless, he started his journey with courage and determination. He warned those who would follow him that following him would require sacrifice, and there wasn't time for second thoughts or to be indecisive.

Our first reading was chosen to correspond with the idea of total commitment to one's call. It tells about two

Old Testament prophets, Elijah and Elisha, who lived about 850 years before Christ. Elijah was getting old and his life was coming to an end. At God's command he chose Elisha to replace him. Elisha was busy farming and Elijah came up to him and placed his mantle on Elisha's shoulders. This gesture symbolized God's call – that Elisha should replace Elijah. It would be similar to my taking off my vestment and putting it over someone's shoulders. The point would be obvious. The reading tells us Elijah had 12 yoke of oxen which would indicate that Elisha must have been quite a prosperous farmer. When he sacrificed his animals and burned his equipment, he was indicating his total commitment to his vocation. He broke completely with his former way of life and did not look back.

HOMILY – A man rushed into the jewelry store one morning and said he needed a pair of diamond earrings right away. The clerk showed him several pairs and immediately he picked out a pair. The clerk asked if he wanted them gift wrapped. The man said, "That would be great, but make it quick. I forgot today is the anniversary of my wife and me and right now she thinks I'm taking out the trash!" (*Reader's Digest - Laughter the Best Medicine*, pg 68) Time was short for the man to get home with his wife's present. Time was short for Jesus too. He knew well what was ahead for him, and he couldn't even wait for a man to bury his father. I often wondered if the situation was such that the man's father was fairly healthy and it might have been many years before his father would die. Jesus didn't have that much time.

Our gospel today begins by telling us Jesus was determined to journey to Jerusalem. He knew what to expect when he got there. He predicted: "it is impossible that a prophet should die outside of Jerusalem." (Lk. 13:33) We heard him in last week's gospel telling his disciples that he would suffer greatly, be rejected and be killed and on the third day be raised. For the next four and a half months, every Sunday gospel will fit within St. Luke's framework of what is called Jesus' "journey narrative." His journey would take him through Samaria, which as we hear in today's gospel, was not very friendly toward the Jews. James and John wanted to punish the Samaritans who did not welcome them, but that was not Jesus' way of doing things. The Samaritans would be the losers because they rejected Jesus. Who knows how many of their sick citizens might have been healed, or how many pearls of wisdom Jesus may have left with them if they had welcomed him. Next we have three sayings of Jesus that emphasize the attitudes that are required from those who would follow him, attitudes requiring sacrifice, sometimes sacrificing our comfort, pleasure and worldly security, sometimes having to put family obligations aside to honor our obligation to God, and always knowing we have to make time for our responsibility to obey and honor God.

This week our nation celebrates its freedom. Unfortunately, in the minds of many people today, freedom means doing whatever you want. If everyone could do whatever they wanted, there would be anarchy and not freedom. St. Paul says today, "you were called for freedom." He goes on to make sure we know freedom is not giving in to every urge or impulse we experience. Freedom is being free to do whatever you should. The freedom we fought for was the freedom to be able to live up to our responsibilities and obligations as we saw them and not as some king or queen saw them. God knows we need laws to guide us and he has given us a few. The framers of our Constitution who fought for our freedom knew we needed laws too. You may have heard the famous quote by James Madison (*Federalist 51*) who said:

"if men were angels, no government would be necessary." You may not have heard the rest of it where he said: "in framing a government which is to be administered by men over men, the great difficulty lies in this: you must first enable the government to control the governed; and in the next place oblige it to control itself."

Among the freedoms we enjoy is freedom of religion. Our Constitution say: "Congress shall make no law respecting an establishment of religion, or prohibiting the free exercise thereof." The Supreme Court has consistently held that the right to free exercise is not absolute. For example Mormons may not practice polygamy. A devotee of paganism cannot initiate human sacrifice. We live in a time where there are those who want to put more restrictions on the exercise of Christianity in general and Catholicism in particular. Just to name a few examples: a human fetus is not human enough to be guaranteed the right to life, a Catholic college like Notre Dame or Xavier is not religious enough to qualify as a religious organization in the Affordable Care Act. We are soon going to be taxed by being required to pay for birth control and for abortion inducing drugs, even though we are conscientiously opposed to them. The IRS will see to it. And what is one to make of the Supreme Court decision this week on marriage? There are many in our society who have no time for religion, who claim no religious affiliation and who consider religion useless, superstitious, antiquated, authoritarian and even harmful. As a people of faith and as a nation we believe that freedom is an unalienable right given by our Creator. As we have had to defend our freedom as a nation many times in order to preserve it, we have to defend our freedom as religious people and it is our right to do so. Amen.

Feast of St. Peter & St. Paul
June 29, 2008

INTRODUCTION – (Acts 12: 1-11, 2 Timothy 4: 6-8, 17-18, Matthew 16:13-19) **At 4:00 Mass:** Christ continues to feed and guide his people through the apostles. We see today how he does this through two of them, Peter and Paul. Peter, in today's first reading, shows us Jesus at work through him and John in healing a person crippled from birth. Peter's position as leader and chief shepherd of God's people is recognized in today's gospel. This was written long after Peter had been put to death, so it is not just Peter who is appointed chief shepherd, but those who would succeed him. We hear from St. Paul in the second reading. Paul was a powerful teacher and his mission was, to a large part, to the Gentiles. He recognized that fidelity to Christ did not require Gentiles to observe all of Jewish law with its feasts and rituals and sacrifices and dietary requirements. In today's second reading he is assuring his readers that he teaches with divine authority and has received backing from Peter (Cephas) and the other leaders of the early Church.

At Sunday Masses: A society cannot survive without structure, organization and authority. Today's feast of the apostles, Peter and Paul, especially today's gospel, reminds us of the way Christ structured his Church with Peter as the head. When we hear this gospel, it might be worth knowing that it was written after Peter had already been put to death. St. Matthew wants us to know that it was a leadership position Jesus was creating when he made Peter the rock and gave him the keys of the kingdom. It was not just a personal prerogative of Peter's. If it were personal only to Peter, who was dead by the time Matthew was writing, why would St. Matthew have made so much of it in his gospel?

I would like you to notice also in today's readings the theme of God helping those who put their trust in him. The first reading tells us how God rescued Peter from prison. The psalm that follows is the prayer of a person praising God for rescuing them from fear and danger. We could easily imagine Peter praying this psalm as he left prison. In the second reading Paul realizes he is approaching the end of his life and he praises God for all the ways he has been protected during his ministry.

HOMILY – Today we celebrate the feast of Saints Peter and Paul. It is a very ancient feast going back to around the year 250 A.D. The two are honored because they are the two apostles about whom we know the most. They were the greatest influence on the Church at its beginning. Tradition has it they died together in Rome during the persecution of the Emperor Nero. Most historians suspect that Nero himself started the fire that burned most of Rome in order to clear out old houses and buildings to make room for his own ambitious building projects. Then he blamed the fire on the Christians in order to take suspicion off himself.

Peter was crucified upside down, again tradition has it that he did not consider himself worthy of dying in the same way his Master had died. Paul was beheaded. Although he was a Jew, he also was legally, by birth, a Roman citizen. Roman law decreed that Roman citizens could not be crucified because it was such a horrific way to die and being exempt from crucifixion was one of the perks of being a Roman citizen.

This year the spotlight is on St. Paul because the Holy Father proclaimed that the rest of this year and the first six months of next year be a year in honor of St. Paul. No one knows when he was born exactly, but scholars figure it was roughly 2000 years ago (give or take three or four years). So we are celebrating his 2000th birthday as closely as we can figure it.

We don't know if Paul ever saw Jesus in the flesh. Paul was born in Tarsus, a city in Asia Minor, which is now modern day Turkey. He spoke Greek and Aramaic and wrote all of his letters in Greek. He was a Pharisee and 1000% dedicated to observance of Jewish law and traditions. Sometime after the death and resurrection of Jesus, he began persecuting the early followers of Christ. He was present at the martyrdom of St. Steven, the first martyr. He viewed those who believed in Jesus as heretics. He was such a zealous devotee to the Jewish Law that he would go looking for believers in Jesus to arrest them and prosecute them. It was on such a journey to Damascus that the Risen Christ spoke to Paul. Paul was enveloped in a bright light and fell to the ground. There is no mention of a horse, although people are used to saying he was thrown off his horse. This idea came from a painting of the event. I rather believe Paul was walking or riding a donkey, which was the usual means of transportation. He heard someone call him, and when he asked who was calling him, Jesus answered: "I am Jesus whom you are persecuting." Then Jesus said: "Now get up and go into the city and you will be told what you must do." Paul got up but he was a new man. He was ill and blind for a few days until he was healed by one of Jesus' followers and was baptized. In his encounter with Jesus, he discovered Jesus was not a heretic and condemned criminal, but the glorified Lord who has risen from the dead and lives in his Church. He would learn that his mission would be to the Gentiles and that the good news Jesus proclaimed was to be preached to all people. This is when Paul became an Apostle for the word Apostle means one who has been sent. He would come to understand how we are saved by Jesus' death and resurrection and by our incorporation into this saving event through three things: 1) faith, 2) the sacraments, especially baptism and the Eucharist and 3) our love for one another.

Paul wrote more than any other New Testament author. One could keep on talking about him because he wrote so much. There is an insert in today's bulletin that says more about Paul. But to put everything succinctly, Paul's life and mission can be summed up in the one sentence Jesus spoke to him on the way to Damascus:

"I am Jesus whom you are persecuting."

As I conclude, we might recall the most famous lines Paul wrote: "love is kind, love is patient, love is not jealous, it is not pompous, etc." ending with the sentence: "love never fails." The kind of love Paul talks about is a love that is rooted in Christ. We express that love as we gather here in faith today, giving God our time and worship and praying for one another. May we continue to express that same love for one another throughout the coming week.

14th Sunday in Ordinary Time
July 7, 2013

INTRODUCTION – (Isaiah 66:10-14; Gal. 6:14-18; Luke 10:1-12, 17-20) Our first reading deals with a time in Jewish history right after the Babylonian exile. After the Jews had been slaves and exiles for 50 years, they were allowed to return home. They didn't return all at once. What they found when they did return was discouraging and depressing. Their cities, lands and homes were in ruins. God encouraged them with messages of comfort and hope through the prophet

Isaiah. He assured them he did not bring them home from exile to abandon them. Jerusalem would be like a mother once again, nurturing them and caring for them. They must rejoice. They will enjoy prosperity once more. The psalm refrain echoes this call to rejoice.

HOMILY – I want to start off asking you to take a couple of deep breaths. That's a good way to relax, but don't fall asleep yet. Now take a deep breath and hold it. Keep holding as long as you can. Few people can do it for longer than a minute. Now you can let it out. We know that it is normal for us to have to breathe in and breathe out. I wanted you to do this to illustrate that this is the way our faith works too. We breathe in all that God has for us, in prayer, in Scripture, in the sacraments, in support from fellow believers and in the many ways God helps us. But we need to breathe out the love and mercy of God and be willing to share our faith with others. The gospel tells us Jesus gathered together 72 disciples and sent them out. He had the Apostles, but the 12 of them were not enough for what he wanted to do. He remarked the harvest is abundant but the laborers are few. (idea came from the June, 2013 publication of *The Word Among Us*.) We pray for vocations at every Mass, but even if we have twice as many priests or religious, we would need you. How can you breathe out God's love and mercy? First through prayer, prayer for those no longer going to Church and also that our Church might grow through membership. We don't have to go out and preach on the street corner, but we can witness effectively through sharing how God has blessed us personally. Some people may think you are a little weird if you do that; they may turn their back on you; they may point out to you all the faults the Church has or faults you may have. Jesus said to the 72, "I am sending you like lambs among wolves." He could see he was being rejected and he knew his followers would be too. St. Luke's community (for whom Luke wrote his gospel 50 years later) was probably experiencing the same rejection and that's why Luke quotes Jesus here. Apparently the 72 on this mission didn't run into hardly any wolves who wanted to tear them apart because they came back rejoicing and telling of their successes. It wouldn't always be that way, unfortunately. There were lots of martyrs in the early Church.

We live in a Country where we should be able to practice our religion freely. But there are those who want to put limits on the exercise of our faith. We just ended a two week period of prayer for religious freedom. The bishops called for a holy hour once a month (we have two a week), they called for a daily rosary and prayers at Mass. They encourage sacrifice such as giving up meat on Fridays. For what purpose are we praying for religious freedom? Against our conscience, our government wants us to pay not only for contraceptives but also for abortion inducing drugs. When the Church asked for an exemption to this mandate, the government decided who is religious enough to be granted an exemption. Some Catholic social services in other areas of our nation have had to give up their work with adoptions and foster care because, in the conscience of the Catholic social service agencies, a child should be placed in a stable family where there is a mother and father who are married to one another. The government put them out of the adoption and foster care business. There are more things; however, I talked about these issues and others this past July 4th, and I don't want to be repetitious. This is another area where we can witness to our faith. We can let our legislators know what we think about the restrictions the government desires to put on our freedom of religion. It is our right to voice our opinion and if enough people speak up, they pay attention.

One last item I want to mention. After Mass today, we will have the anointing of the sick. Jesus healed the sick and in today's gospel he sent the 72 out to exorcise demons and to heal the sick. In this way they would proclaim the coming of the kingdom of God, a kingdom in which there would be no more suffering, no more evil, no more sickness and death. Jesus is calling us to eternal life with him. He depends on us to get the word out. Amen.

15th Sunday in Ordinary Time
July 14, 2013

INTRODUCTION – (Deut 30:10-14; Colossians 1:15-20; Luke 10:25-37) The Book of Deuteronomy is a series of sermons addressed to the people of Israel by Moses right before they were to enter the Promised Land. Moses had led them from the slavery of Egypt and was with them for many years as they traveled through the Sinai desert. Moses knew he would die before the people could enter their Promised Land, so he is in a sense giving them some last words of wisdom before he would have to leave them. Today's first reading begins with an incomplete sentence: "If only you would heed the voice of the Lord " The sentence implies that God would bless them greatly "if only they would heed the voice of the Lord " The passage goes on to stress that people do not have to guess what God wants of them. It's no hidden mystery. This concept connects with today's gospel – the story of the good Samaritan. The story is depicted in our stained glass window by the door on the Blessed Virgin side. When a scholar of the law asked Jesus what God wants of us, Jesus' reply to the man shows that the man already knew the answer to his question.

Almost instinctively, we all know what God wants of all of us. Knowing it is not the problem; living it is.

HOMILY – A scholar of the law asked Jesus a question about what God expects of us: "Teacher, what must I do to inherit eternal life." In other places in the Scriptures, Jesus himself always answered this question. Perhaps on this occasion, Jesus understood the person asking the question knew the answer, so Jesus asked him what the law said. The answer the lawyer gave to his own question is an answer we all know – to love God with our whole being and to love our neighbor as much as we love ourselves . The part about loving our neighbor is not just a Jewish law; it is what all religions believe in. It is called the golden rule: "do unto others as you would have them do unto you."

In the time of Jesus, love of neighbor applied only to fellow Israelites. Eventually this law of love was extended also to foreigners living in Israel (Deut 10:19) but not to others. Jesus, who came to save all people, gave an interpretation to this commandment of love that is as broad as possible: it extends even to loving one's enemies. (Mt. 6:43 ff) Indeed, his story about the Good Samaritan illustrated this. To the Jewish mind, no Samaritan was good. There was hostility between the Jews and the Samaritans that went back for hundreds of years. This is an example of their mutual hostility. Jews traveling from Galilee to Jerusalem would normally avoid Samaria which was right between both places. They would bypass Samaria by crossing the Jordan river and then going into the area that is today the country of Jordan. They would then go south and cross the river again to go thru Jericho to make the 18 mile long climb up to Jerusalem. It surely added a day or two to their trip. This road to Jerusalem ascended from 770 feet below sea level to 2500 feet above and it was a treacherous and dangerous road. It was on this road between Jericho and Jerusalem that our story of the Good Samaritan takes place.

We have become familiar and comfortable with this story of Jesus, but it would have shocked the people of Jesus' time who heard it. If we were to retell the story to ourselves today, we would have to change the characters: for example, the first person who passed the victim of violence would be a bishop, then the next person would be a priest, and finally the third person, who helped the victim, would be a member of the Moslem Brotherhood. That puts a different light on the story doesn't it?

Notice when the Scriptures talk about love, they don't refer to warm, fuzzy feelings, (which may or may not occur in conjunction with love), but in talking of love, the Scriptures talk about what it is we do to honor and obey God and to care for one another. The last line of the gospel tells us to "go and do likewise!" Today's gospel message on love is a lifetime task. With inspiration from Jesus, who has shown us great love, and with the help of the Holy Spirit, may we continue to grow in God's love. Amen.

16th Sunday in Ordinary Time
July 21, 2013

INTRODUCTION – (Genesis 18:1-10; Colossians 1:24-28; Luke 10:38-42) God is always with us, but there are those times when God's presence becomes tangible. It's always a surprise when it happens. Sometimes God's visits come in the form of a good idea or with a strong awareness that we're not alone. Sometimes they come with a deep sense of peace or with a twinge of conscience. And, of course, God comes to visit us as our life in this world reaches its end.

Our first reading is about Abraham who welcomes three strangers. Abraham didn't realize at first that it was God whom he was entertaining. God had come to tell him that his lifelong desire that he and his wife, Sarah, would have a son would finally be fulfilled. Our first reading prepares us for the story of Martha and Mary (illustrated by our stained glass window) as these two sisters are visited by Jesus – whom they had not yet come to know was the Son of God, the giver of every blessing, and the One who spoke words of eternal life.

HOMILY – I would like to begin with last week's gospel. It is connected with today's. If you will recall, a scholar in the Jewish law asked Jesus a question: "what must I do to inherit eternal life?" Could there be a more important question in our lives than this one? And yet, it's a question a lot of people in our society do not seem to have much concern. Somehow many people figure we are all going to be saved in the end, no matter how we've lived. That's not the message we get from the gospel. Once Jesus was asked: "Lord, will only a few be saved?" Jesus answered: "strive to enter through the narrow door, for many, I tell you, will try to enter and will not be able." (Lk. 13:23-24). We would be considering Jesus a fool or a liar if we did not take seriously the many parables Jesus spoke regarding the importance of being ready to enter God's kingdom.

To get the answer to the question: "what must I do to inherit eternal life?" Jesus asked the scholar in Jewish law what he thought was the answer. Of course, the scholar answered correctly: to love God with our whole heart and soul and mind and strength and to love our neighbor as ourselves. Then he asked Jesus for a definition of neighbor, which led into the parable of the Good Samaritan.

I feel sure that St. Luke put today's gospel right after the story about the Good Samaritan for a reason. It is an illustration of the first and greatest commandment: to love God with our whole heart and soul and mind and strength. The story of Martha and Mary does not imply that Martha did not love God, while Mary did. Martha loved God too. She was demonstrating her love by getting a big meal together for Jesus and the twelve apostles. But Jesus told her, "you are busy (the Greek word also means "distracted") about many things." While the gospel of the good Samaritan tells us to care about one another (which is what Martha was doing), Jesus tells us sometimes we have to stop being busy and give him our undivided attention (and that is what Mary was doing). Another word for that is "prayer." In other words, we need to pray as well as do good works to be a good disciple.

Whenever most people think of prayer, they think of "saying prayers." That is a good way to pray, but we can also pray by listening, thinking about what Christ has taught us, or just being with Christ and giving him our attention without saying or thinking anything. That's what Mary was doing. That's what Jesus was suggesting to Martha she try doing and to stop being so busy all the time. "Martha, Martha, you are worried and distracted about many things (meaning too many things) there is need of only one thing." The story is telling us that in our busy lives, we need to make some time to spend with God.

We do call Sunday the Lord's Day and that's why we are here. Thank you for making time for God today. These days, on the Lord's Day, the Lord is fortunate to get even a minute's thought from some people. Fulfilling our Sunday obligation is the first and most important way we are to express our total love of God for the Mass is the greatest prayer we have, the most perfect act of worship we can offer God. In my own spiritual life, besides the Mass and the Divine Office which I say every day and my weekly holy hour. I mention these things simply as an illustration of the various ways we can pray. I enjoy studying the Scriptures daily, I say the rosary frequently, and every day I just sit quietly in church for a while. I talk to God about whatever comes to my mind, or I just listen for him to speak. Some people pray through singing hymns or the psalms. I assure you my daily prayers have been a great blessing for me throughout my life. I believe the hardest thing about prayer is making time for it. When I feel as if I'm too busy to pray, I always say to myself: if you don't schedule it in, you schedule it out. So I schedule it in. I often recommend that people who do not go to Mass on Sundays should sit down and pray for an hour so they stay in touch with God. Prayer is as important for our relationship with God as communication is for our relationships with one another. Amen.

17th Sunday in Ordinary Time
July 28, 2013

INTRODUCTION – (Genesis 18:20-32; Col. 2:12-14; Luke 11:1-13) We heard last Sunday about Abraham having a surprise visit from three strangers. Abraham provided a feast for them and as it turned out one of the three visitors was God himself. God revealed he was greatly displeased with two cities near the Dead Sea, Sodom and Gomorrah, and he invited Abraham to go with him as he went to visit them. Abraham realized God was about to severely punish those cities for their depravity and immorality, and he shows his concern because his nephew, Lot, lived in Sodom. Notice the comfortable, yet respectful, familiarity that existed between God and Abraham.

HOMILY – Psychologically, we often relate to God, our Father in heaven, in ways that are similar to the ways we related to our father here on earth. My father was a good provider, and I think that has served to help me trust in God as a good provider, but my father was not like God in encouraging me to keep on asking if I wanted something. I had a strict father and I don't know how many times I heard him say: "I told you once and I don't want to tell you again: NO, you can't do this or you can't have that." When he said NO he meant it and don't dare ask again. In today's gospel, Jesus tells us to persist in asking. It's not because God doesn't know what we want or need, or he's too busy to care about our needs right now, but our persistence helps to create a dialogue and build a relationship with him. Every prayer will be heard, and every prayer will bring us a blessing, even if it's not the exact thing we want. If we don't get the exact thing we want, it means he has something better in mind. No prayer is ever be wasted. One of the things all the saints stress is that we should never quit praying, even when we're not in the mood, because that's when our relationship with God and our faith grow deeper. Amen.

18th Sunday in Ordinary Time
August 5, 2007

INTRODUCTION – (Eccl 1:2, 2:21-23; Col 3:1-5, 9-11; Luke 12:13-21) Today's first reading comes from one of the wisdom books in the Old Testament. This book is sometimes called by its Hebrew title, Qoheleth. The name means simply "one who convenes an assembly." The author was probably a teacher or preacher. When the name Qoheleth is translated into the Greek, it comes out Ecclesiastes. It's a book we hear from only once in the three-year Sunday cycle of readings. And it's a short passage at that. Most of us are familiar with another passage in Qoheleth that begins: "For everything there is a season...a time for every matter under heaven. A time to be born and a time to die, and so on...." Today's passage reminds us of the passing nature of all things.

HOMILY – A sign outside of church announced: "Don't wait for the hearse to take you to church." Today's gospel shows us the folly of failing to grow rich spiritually. It's the only thing that's will outlast everything else. Billy Graham once pointed out "You never see a hearse pulling a U-Haul trailer." When the richest man in a town died, the local news reporter asked his pastor, "how much did he leave." The pastor replied, "All of it!"

Qoheleth said "All things are vanity." The Hebrew word used here for "vanity" means something without substance, something like a puff of smoke. If you read the book of Qoheleth, you get the impression that the author enjoyed all the best things life had to offer: pleasure, wealth, power and knowledge. Yet he found nothing of lasting value or satisfaction. The conclusion of this book tells us to enjoy each day as it comes and not become too attached to anything this world has to offer. It was a practical way of looking at life considering Jewish faith at this time in history had not yet come to a faith in the existence of heaven or hell, reward or punishment. They believed in a kind of existence after death, but it was an existence that was neither happy nor unhappy. With whatever information he had, Qoheleth's conclusion to just enjoy each day as it comes was the best idea anyone could come up with. But Jesus has more to offer. Jesus offers us something that is lasting. Jesus called the rich farmer a "fool" in today's parable, because the farmer thought he was set for life, he had all he needed. He was wealthy in worldly goods but he did not grow rich in the sight of God. The word "fool" here means someone with limited thinking, someone without good sense! St. Paul gives us the same message in today's second reading: "Think of what is above, not of what is on earth."

The parable Jesus gives us follows a few comments he made about greed and how dangerous it is. Greed certainly is dangerous. It is one of the capital sins and gives rise to things like cheating, stealing, lying, quarreling, fighting and even war. It doesn't sound as if the farmer did any of these bad things. It sounds as if he made his fortune by good weather and good old fashioned hard work. Is Jesus saying it is sinful to be rich and successful? Jesus seems to be saying it is a sin if that is our main focus in life, if we build our security only on the things this world can give us, if we forget where our blessings come from. It is also a sin to be rich if our hearts are cold to the sufferings of those not so fortunate as we are. I'm not trying to make anyone here feel guilty about not giving a buck to every bum who asks for it. I don't do that myself and I don't feel guilty about it, because I know, from past experience, most of the people who got money out of me were just con artists. I tend to let legitimate agencies, which I support, help the really poor. Going back to the rich farmer, he forgot he was not in control. He owned so much he thought he owned the future and he didn't. He didn't know he had no future and all his wealth would be left behind. His priorities were wrong, Jesus said. There are two remedies that help us keep our priorities in balance. First of all there is the third commandment, which tells us to keep holy the Lord's day. Honoring God reminds us of who God is and that we owe God everything we have and everything we are. Secondly there's a remedy to help us not forget about the needs of others. It's called tithing.

Giving away some of our money reminds us it's not all ours. (10% was required of the Jewish people.) It keeps us aware that what we have has been given to us in the first place. People like to say, "I earned it." Maybe so, but where did we get the health, the talent, the energy, the education, the opportunities to earn it. That was all given to us. We do have to provide for ourselves and our families and we have to save for that proverbial rainy day, but we can't become totally selfish either. That's greed. We have to keep things in balance and loving God and loving our neighbor is part of the balance.

You've heard this story before, but it's worth repeating. An American tourist, traveling in Europe, paid a visit to a famous wise and holy rabbi who lived there. The American was surprised when he saw how simply the man lived – in a single room with only books and a table and chair. "Rabbi! Where is your furniture?" asked the tourist. "Where is yours?" the rabbi asked. The American tourist answered, "My furniture? I'm only passing through here." The wise rabbi responded: "So am I!"

19th Sunday in Ordinary Time
August 12, 2007

INTRODUCTION – (Wis 18:6-9; Heb 11:1-2, 8-19; Luke 12:32-48) The spiritual tradition we follow as Christians did not begin with Christ. It began long before Christ as God prepared the world for the coming of Christ through the Jewish people. Our two readings take us back in history to our spiritual beginning. Today's second reading takes us back to the time of

Abraham, almost 19 centuries before Christ. Abraham and his wife Sarah were the parents of the Jewish people. The letter to the Hebrews puts Abraham and Sarah before us as models of faith for us to imitate. The first reading takes us several centuries after the time of Abraham to the time when God's people, in faith, left Egypt to head for the Promised Land under the leadership of Moses.

HOMILY – We were introduced to the faith of Abraham and Sarah as they left their homeland and relatives to travel to a new land where God was leading them. They had faith too in God's promise they would have many descendants even as they were without children and were growing older. We were introduced to the faith of the Jewish people as they set out under the leadership of Moses, leaving behind an unpleasant life of slavery for a more uncertain journey through desert and wilderness to an unknown land.

Each of us today is making his or her own journey. It might be toward graduation from school, it might be toward marriage or toward a new career, it might be toward improved health, it might be toward retirement or it might be just a matter of trying to survive the stresses of each day. Whatever it is, time is moving us along. We are unable to stand still in life, and if we try, we'll eventually discover that we're going backwards. We know from everyday experience that if it's a better place we are moving toward, we need to adequately prepare ourselves for it.

In our journey through life, there is an event that we definitely need to prepare for. That is the day we are going to meet our Lord, not just in prayer, not just in the sacraments, not just in the invisible ways in which he comes into our lives, but in a visible, unmistakable way at the end of life's journey through this life. It's a meeting most of us like to put off as long as possible and many people do not like to even think about. That's why our Lord warns us to prepare for it, because we may tend to procrastinate or just put it out of our minds altogether.

Jesus uses two simple examples. The first is about the head of a household who was out of town for a wedding celebration. In Jesus' day wedding celebrations often went on for days, so it's understandable that the servants would not know when to expect their master's return. The second is about a thief. Of course, a thief doesn't warn a person before breaking into their house. If Jesus were preaching today, he might use the example of terrorism. We're sadly familiar with the havoc it can cause and the need to be diligently on the alert. Unlike a thief or a terrorist who may be prevented from striking, Jesus' coming is not a matter of if but of when.

The reason he warns us is not to fill us with fear, but because he loves us and he wants us to share in all the blessings he has for us. If we're not ready, we may miss out. Most of God's people who left Egypt started off with faith, but when the going got difficult they refused to do the things God told them and they missed out on enjoying the blessings of the Promised Land. I am sure many people here have seen the sign which said, "Jesus is coming. Try to look busy!" Being prepared is not something we can fake or make happen at the last second. It's the way we live our lives in faith and love. Faith and love are not superficial attitudes that have no substance. They are attitudes that guide us to live our life every day the way Jesus taught us.

Right now we follow the lead Jesus gave us as we do in his memory what he commanded us, worshiping the Father through our sharing in his perfect sacrifice. Amen.

20th Sunday in Ordinary Time
August 18, 2013

INTRODUCTION – (Jeremiah 38:4-6, 8-10; Hebrews 12:1-4; Luke 12:49-53) Suffering and turmoil have been part of everyday life in the Middle East for centuries. Our first reading goes back 600 years before Christ when the land we now know as Iraq was known as Babylon. It was during that time that Nebuchadnezzar, the king of Babylon, was successfully conquering all the nations that surrounded Babylon. The events we will hear in our first reading took place as the Babylonians were attacking Jerusalem. Jeremiah, one of the greatest prophets of all time, kept telling the Jewish leaders as well as anyone who would listen to him that it was useless for them to defend themselves; they should just surrender to the Babylonians or Jerusalem would be destroyed. Such talk was viewed as unpatriotic and Jeremiah was called a traitor. Many of the Jewish leaders decided to kill Jeremiah and they persuaded their king, Zedekiah, to get rid of the prophet. Zedekiah gave permission for Jeremiah to be thrown into a cistern to die. Later, Ebed-Melech, a Cushite (which means an Ethiopian), one of Jeremiah's friends, persuaded the king to change his mind.

HOMILY – Today's readings are not cheerful. First we heard of Jeremiah who was faithful to God in every way and who spoke God's message to God's people. He was rewarded by being thrown down a cistern and left to die. I'm sure some of us feel like Jeremiah at times. By the way, Jeremiah was correct. Because of the resistance of the Jews, the Babylonians completely destroyed Jerusalem and that led to the Babylonian Exile.

In the gospel we hear of Jesus, THE greatest prophet ever. Luke tells us Jesus was on his way to Jerusalem knowing fully well what was ahead for him. Jesus described this in three ways: as a fire he wished to cast upon the earth, as a baptism he was to receive, and that he would be a cause of division. The fire and baptism he spoke of are vague: (1) fire can symbolize judgment, purification or discernment. It also could symbolize the fire of the Holy Spirit that came upon the apostles at Pentecost. What Jesus meant by fire is unclear. (2) Jesus also spoke of a baptism he would undergo. This is a strange symbol for Jesus to use, especially since he had already received the baptism of John the Baptist. The baptism he was to receive might be clearer if we recall that once Jesus referred to his suffering and death as a baptism when he asked James and John, two apostles who wanted the highest places of honor in God's kingdom, "can you drink the cup that I am to drink or be baptized with the baptism that I shall undergo?" If baptism and fire are difficult to understand, we have no difficulty understanding Jesus when he talks about (3) the division that he would create. "Do you think that I have come to establish peace on the earth? No, I tell you, but rather division." This word foretold the sufferings and even the martyrdom some of his followers would experience. Here Jesus focused specifically on division within families for family bonds were one of the strongest and most sacred bonds in the society of Jesus' time. The example of division that Jesus chose illustrates that membership in God's kingdom was even more important than family ties.

Didn't Jesus come to bring peace? Certainly! At his birth the angels sang "glory to God in the highest, and peace on earth to people of good will." When Jesus sent his disciples out on mission, they were instructed that when they entered a person's house they were to say: "Peace to this house." At the Last Supper he promised his disciples a "peace which the world cannot give."

After his resurrection, his first words to the disciples when he appeared to them were: "Peace be with you." The greatest source of peace in my life is my relationship with God. Peace is more than just the absence of war, it is a figure for the many blessings that he and his ministry would bring to human beings. (Fitzmyer, *Anchor Bible*, pg 225) So when Jesus speaks of division, he is speaking of the ongoing battle between good and evil, between those who believe and follow him and those who reject him. It is Jesus' intention to offer God's forgiveness and love to all who would accept it. Division results from the fact that there will always be those who resist Jesus' offer.

This battle can go on even within our own selves – with part of us wanting to love God and follow his ways and a part of us wanting to go in the opposite direction. The second reading today from Hebrews encourages us to persevere in running the race and keeping our eyes fixed on Jesus for he is the true source of a peace that will have no end.

We come here today with our challenges, our worries and struggles, whether within ourselves, or with our relatives or our neighbors, or our politicians or the world at large. Typically, we work to achieve some peace and stability in our lives, but I suppose there will always be challenges. So we come to our Lord for strength and guidance, for his love and for his peace. Amen.

Vigil & Feast of the Assumption
August 14/15, 2010

INTRODUCTION – People often confuse the Ascension and the Assumption. The Ascension commemorates Jesus ascending into heaven and taking his place at the right hand of God. It is celebrated on the

Seventh Sunday of Easter. The Assumption commemorates our belief that Mary, after her life on this earth had come to an end, was raised up to eternal life and was taken into heaven, body and soul. It was only fitting that she who was Jesus' mother and who was full of grace her entire life, should share first, before all others, in the risen glory of her Son. The dogma of the Assumption was declared by Pope Pius XII in 1950, but it had been believed and celebrated for centuries before that.

Vigil Mass: Our first reading (1 Chronicles 15:3-4, 15-16; 16:1-2) is about the Ark of the Covenant, the sacred gold-plated box that contained the Ten Commandments. The Ark was the unique symbol of God's presence with Israel. It was constructed in the desert by Moses on the way to the Promised Land. When King David established his capital in Jerusalem about the year 1000 BC, he brought the Ark there. Today's reading describes this solemn and joyful occasion. In Christian symbolism, Mary is sometimes referred to as the Ark of the Covenant. Just as God was present in a special way wherever the Ark was taken, so God was present with Mary in a most special way when she carried within her womb the only Son of God, Jesus our Savior. The early Christians also saw Jerusalem as a symbol of heaven. That symbolism is reflected in today's first reading. The Ark being taken up to Jerusalem symbolizes Mary being taken body and soul into the heavenly kingdom.

Mass during the day: Our first reading (Revelation 11:19a, 12:1-6a, 10ab) is from the book of Revelation. The book of Revelation is highly symbolic. Some of the symbolism is quite obvious while it requires a fairly extensive knowledge of Scripture to interpret some of the other symbols. In today's first reading we hear about a woman, a child and a dragon. The dragon represents the devil and the powers of evil at work in the world.

The child is Christ. The woman in our reading has a double symbolism. She stands for Mary, the physical mother of Jesus Christ, and she stands for the Church, our spiritual mother who brings Jesus Christ to birth in us through faith and the sacraments. In today's passage the woman is rescued from the powers of the dragon and is described in great glory. This too has a double symbolism. It symbolizes the glory of Mary in the assumption. It also symbolizes God's faithful people whom he will rescue from evil and will bring, in the resurrection from the dead, into the glory of heaven.

HOMILY – Mary's assumption into heavenly glory is not explicitly described in the Scriptures. As St. John says at the end of his gospel, the Scriptures do not tell us everything that could be said about Jesus, what he said or did, much less does it tell us everything about Mary or the Apostles or the early Church. The Church has believed for centuries that Mary was so honored in the assumption because no one followed Christ as perfectly as she did, thus it is perfectly appropriate that Mary would follow him into eternal glory, body and soul.

A painting by Raphael (Vatican Pinacoteca: Crowning of the Virgin – Oddi Altarpice) recalls the legend that when Mary's life came to an end, the apostles buried her. Thomas, however, was not there at the time and when he returned he wanted to see for himself that she had died. When they opened her tomb, her body was gone. It had been raised and was taken to heaven by her Son who crowned her as queen. St. Francis de Sales said: "What son would not bring his mother back to life and would not bring her into paradise after her death if he could?" Actually, no one knows where Mary might have passed away – whether it was in Jerusalem or in Ephesus. Another painting by Raphael (Vatican Pinacoteca: Madonna of Foligno) is one I thought was very lovely. It is part of a larger piece which includes St. John the Baptist and St. Francis on the left and St. Jerome introducing the kneeling Sigismondo Conti who was the patron who commissioned the painting.

Homily ending at Vigil Mass: We celebrate the honor and privilege given to Mary. Today, in Mary, we also celebrate our hope of final glorification when Christ will raise up to new life all those who have followed him faithfully. In the gospel a woman from the crowd called Mary blessed, but Jesus reminds us why she was truly blessed, in that she "heard God's word and obeyed it."

Homily ending at Mass during the day: Mary praised God in her visit to Elizabeth: "The Almighty has done great things for me, and holy is his name." Today we celebrate the honor and privilege given to Mary, but today in Mary we also celebrate our hope of final glorification when Christ will raise up to new life all those who have followed him faithfully. As St. Paul tells us in his wonderful chapter on the resurrection: "For just as in Adam all die, so too in Christ shall all be brought to life but each one in proper order: Christ the first fruits; then, at his coming, those who belong to Christ." No one belonged to Christ as perfectly as Mary did. Amen.

21st Sunday in Ordinary Time
August 25, 2013

INTRODUCTION – (Is. 66:18-21; Hebrews 12:5-7, 11-13; Luke 13:22-30) Our first reading today comes from the time when the Jews were exiled in Babylon. They had been in exile for about two generations by the time God sent to them the prophet we hear from today. By this time the Jews had given up any hope of returning to the land of Judea and to their beloved city, Jerusalem. The prophet tells God's disheartened people they would once again worship in Jerusalem. The prophet foresees a time when even people from foreign nations would join the Jewish people in worshiping the God of Israel. More startling yet, the prophet sees a time when foreigners would be accepted as priests. This was a radical concept. The Jews thought they had a monopoly on God's love and they thought that Gentiles had very little chance for salvation or for sharing in God's kingdom. This question about salvation comes up in today's gospel: who will be saved and how many.

HOMILY – There are two questions that Jesus addresses in today's gospel: who will be saved and how many. Who and how many will share in the bounty of God's kingdom? You will notice, first of all, that Jesus was asked only one question: "Will only a few people be saved?" Jesus was not asked who will be saved because the Jews presumed that Gentiles would be excluded from God's kingdom in the world to come – with the possibility of very few exceptions. So basically, Jesus was really being asked, "will only a few Jews be saved?" Jesus, like Isaiah in the first reading, shocks his listeners by telling them that God's saving love would be made available to all people, all nations. He thus answered a question they hadn't asked him as to who will be saved? As he said toward the end of today's gospel: "many would come from the east and the west, from the north and the south and will recline at table in the kingdom of God," while many of God's own people, the Israelites, would be left outside. That was something Jesus' hearers didn't expect to hear.

Now with this clarification that the Jews had no monopoly on salvation, let us return to the original question at the beginning of today's gospel: "will only a few people be saved?" You may have noticed it was a question Jesus chose not to answer directly. I had often wondered why he didn't. This is pure speculation, but my thoughts as to why he didn't give a direct answer go something like this: suppose for example Jesus had said most of you will be saved. I suspect those who heard this might become very complacent and start thinking: "well I'm a better person than most people so I surely have it made – I don't have to keep trying so hard!" However, what if Jesus said "not many of you will be saved," there would likely be a reaction like this: why try to be good, it's going to be too hard anyway. Put in any number or any percent you want and it would lead to a variety of unhelpful responses that Jesus didn't want to create. What Jesus did want to stress was the important idea that we all have to work hard to enter into the kingdom. We can't take it for granted. We can't think we are entitled to it, no matter who we are or to what group we belong. In today's gospel he said we must strive to enter through the narrow gate. The Greek word translated here as "strive" is αγωνίδζεσθε (agonidzesthe) (you can hear the word "agony" in this word). It would be better translated "strain every nerve, take pains, exert yourself, to enter" That's the indirect answer Jesus gave to his questioner "will only a few be saved?" He said: "Work at it." In other words, as he said on other occasions: "Whoever comes to me listens to my words and acts on them." (Lk. 6:47)

I've thought about another image in today's gospel – the "narrow door." Strive to enter through the narrow door (sometimes it is called a gate, but door is the more accurate word). I have not seen this explanation anywhere, but it struck me the door was narrow because it defined definite boundaries, definite limits to our behavior that fit with what God wants of us. Contrast the narrow door with a big, wide open door that might symbolize doing whatever you feel like doing, no matter what it is or who gets hurt. The wide door symbolized making up our own rules. The narrow door symbolizes living by the values God has taught us and has demanded of us (not just suggested to us) such as: don't cheat or steal, don't lie, don't kill, don't envy, don't use sex inappropriately, keep holy the Lord's day, loving our enemies, do not hold grudges, etc. How many will strive to get through the narrow door and will be able to is a mystery, but Jesus did tell us many will seek to get in and will not be able. I would like to believe, as I'm sure you would too, that everyone is going to go to heaven when they leave this world. That's not what Jesus is telling us.

On vacation I read a couple of the latest books about near death experiences, one called *Heaven is for Real* and the other titled *Proof of Heaven*. They were beautiful books and very inspiring. One can get the impression from some of the accounts of near death experiences that going to heaven is automatic, but I remember years ago reading about near death experiences and some people reported having had experiences that were not good or happy. As I stress that not everyone will be able to pass through the narrow door, I don't want everyone going home depressed, thinking I don't have a chance. Don't forget the book of Revelations gives us a vision of heaven where there was a great multitude that no one could count standing before God's heavenly throne praising him. So even though Jesus said many will be unable to enter, many also will share in God's kingdom – those who chose to make the effort to get through the narrow door.

22nd Sunday in Ordinary Time
September 1, 2013

INTRODUCTION – (Sirach 3:17-18, 20, 28-29; Heb 12:8-19, 22-24a; Luke 14:1, 7-14) A man was sitting at a bar on the top floor of a tall building, having a drink. A second man came in (man #2), sat next to man #1 and started making small talk. In the course of their conversation, he asked man #1 what he was drinking. Man #1 said this is my magic potion. Man #2 inquired what is a magic potion. Man #1 said watch and I'll show you. He got down off the bar stool, walked to the edge of the building and flew around the building, and did a few somersaults as he flew around. He came back to the bar and said that's a magic potion. Man #2 said to the bartender "I'll have one of whatever he's drinking." He downed his drink, walked to the edge of the building, jumped off and went straight down until he crashed on the sidewalk below. The bartender said to man #1, "You know when you've had too much to drink, you're a complete jerk, Superman!" In today's gospel Jesus is talking to people at a dinner who each thought they were Superman, not in the sense that they could fly, but in the sense that they were superior to the rest of the invited guests. As I reflected on today's readings, I thought the most important thing I can talk about today is Jesus' lesson on humility. The capital sin of pride can hurt us in many ways other than just causing us some occasional humiliation or embarrassment. It stands in the way of our relationship with God and with others.

Let me clarify something here before I get too deep into this topic. There is a good kind of pride. It is a healthy pride founded on truth and grounded in reality. It is the recognition of the talents or accomplishments we can lay claim to. If God has given a person certain gifts, such as being able to sing or being very bright and that person denies they have such gifts, "I'm not very smart or I'm just tone deaf" that person is not being humble, they are just mistaken or they just are fishing for compliments, expecting someone to respond: "Don't say that! You are so talented!" Healthy pride also acknowledges that what we have accomplished in life was due to the support and help of others. It is unhealthy pride or neurotic pride that is full of self-love. We blow our talents and accomplishments out of proportion, we convince ourselves we are greater than we really are, we are more important than we really are.

I could speculate that neurotic pride started with our first parents who were told by the devil that if they did what God told them not to do, they would be like God. Bertrand Russell, the philosopher, said: "Every man would like to be God if it were possible; some few find it difficult to admit the impossibility." That's how neurotic pride gets in the way of our relationship with God, because for a proud person, God is someone he or she is competing with rather than a person who is respected, obeyed and loved.

I have learned a lot about humility by learning to laugh at myself. So many times I've seen someone do something stupid and if I'm in a hurry or they annoy me, I think uncomplimentary things about that person. And before I know it I catch myself doing the same thing. Then I just have a good laugh at myself and learn not to be so critical of others when I see them making a mistake. Making mistakes is part of being human. If a person thinks they should be above making mistakes, that's neurotic pride. The irony of it is, when they do make a mistake, their pride comes down on them with a vengeance, telling them they are stupid or worthless or useless or whatever, because they did not live up to the unrealistic degree of perfection they had imagined to themselves that they possessed. This may seem contradictory, but I have found in counseling that often people who are really hard on themselves, angry, hating or blaming themselves, are very prideful persons who set impossible standards for themselves. Certainly we should try to do our best and keep working to improve ourselves, but only God is perfect.

Alex Haley who wrote the novel *Roots* and who was responsible for the highly successful TV series in the 70's said he has in his office a picture of a turtle sitting on a fencepost. He said when he looks at it he remembers a lesson taught to him by a friend who said: "if you see a turtle sitting on top of a fencepost, you know he didn't get there by himself, he had some help getting there." Haley said "anytime I start thinking 'isn't it wonderful the things I've done,' I look at the picture of this turtle and I see myself and I remember I didn't get where I am without a lot of help from others." (*Preaching Resources; Celebration;* Sept 1, 2013)

I thought this story is a good image of humility, recognizing the worth of the talents and accomplishments that we can lay claim to, without forgetting the help and the gifts that have been given to us.

I think one way to gain humility is through prayer. When we fail to pray, we are acting as if we think we can handle things ourselves. When we pray, we are practicing or learning humility because we are reaching out to Another (spelled with a capital "A") to whom we owe all we have and are.

Then there are the hundreds of others too: parents, other relatives, friends, neighbors, co-workers, even people who drive us crazy who have helped to form us and make us who we are. Humility makes us aware we are not the center of the universe, but one small piece of it. That is where the second part of our gospel comes in. Aware that so many have helped us, how can we not reach out to help those who have not been as blessed as we have been. Jesus doesn't mean we are not allowed to invite friends, relatives, neighbors to dinner; I think he says that for emphasis. He just doesn't want us to forget those who do not have the wherewithal to invite us in return. That is also humility. If I can say anything helpful to you today, work to avoid excessive pride. Don't forget the turtle on the fencepost and don't forget to be grateful to God and to the people who brought you to where you are. Amen.

23rd Sunday in Ordinary Time
September 8, 2013

INTRODUCTION – (Wisdom 9:13-18; Philemon: 9-10, 12-17; Luke 14:25-33) To understand our second reading, I need to explain something about slavery in the Roman Empire because Paul's letter is about a slave named Onesimus and prisons because Paul was in prison. First slavery: slavery was common in the Roman Empire but much different than our experience of slavery before the Civil War. Slaves came from nations and peoples that Rome had conquered and most slaves were probably white; many would have been educated and would have worked as musicians, scribes, craftsmen, teachers and even doctors. A slave owner could set any of his or her slaves free or a slave could buy his or her own freedom. Today's second reading is about a slave named Onesimus (a name which means "useful"). Onesimus escaped from his owner, and if he were caught he could have been put to death. Out of desperation he ran to Paul, for he knew Paul and Paul had converted his owner, Philemon, to belief in Christ. Paul was in prison at the time awaiting trial. Regarding prisons, the Romans did not consider it a punishment to give a person a roof over their head and three square meals a day. Prison was just temporary until a Roman magistrate decided the prisoner would be executed, sent into exile, have their property confiscated, or be set free. Often prisoners needed friends or family to provide for their basic needs and, apparently, Onesimus did that for Paul. For Paul, Onesimus lived up to his name: useful. In the process Paul converted him to Christ. Paul thus refers to Onesimus as his own child for he has led him to rebirth in Christ. Paul would have liked to keep Onesimus with him to help him, but he felt an obligation to send him back to Philemon. He didn't feel right benefiting from a gift that had not been given to him. In the letter we hear in today's second reading, Paul asked Philemon to receive Onesimus back, not as property he might own, but as a brother in the Lord. Christianity transcends all of our relationships.

HOMILY – Before I comment on the particular passage I just read, I think today would be a good opportunity to comment on the formation of the gospels in general. Right away, after the resurrection and ascension of Jesus, the small Christian community began to gather to pray, to listen to the instructions of the Apostles and to celebrate the Eucharist – which is what believers have been doing for 2000 years. (Acts 2:42) The community would hear over and over the story of Jesus, his teachings, his marvelous works and his death and resurrection. These stories about Jesus and the breaking of the bread formed their faith and their lives. As the faith spread in various directions and as the Church grew, these stories were written down, but these writings were not yet the gospels as we have them. They were a collection of stories the community wanted to hold on to. I might mention Paul's letters were written earlier than the gospels were. For example, Paul's first letter to the Thessalonians (the earliest of his letter that we have) was written in 50 or 51, while Mark's gospel (the earliest gospel we have) was not written until sometime probably in the early 60's (at least 10 years later). Luke's gospel is dated around 80 to 85 and Matthew's is dated probably in the late 80's, a few years after Luke. Both Luke and Matthew depended on Mark's gospel when they wrote theirs, but Luke and Matthew also have material that Mark does not have. Scholars hypothesize they evidentially borrowed from another source. That source no longer exists, and it is referred to in the literature as Q. Q stands for Quelle – the German word for source.

I said this would be a good Sunday to say all of this because we see evidence of it in today's gospel. Today's gospel involves some very difficult sayings of Jesus. Luke pictures Jesus speaking about the conditions of discipleship – there are three, each ending with the words "cannot be my disciple." The first condition is that one must hate one's father and mother, wife and children, brothers and sisters and even one's own life. A similar saying is in Matthew, but not in Mark, by which scholars conclude that Matthew and Luke got this saying from a source other than Mark, thus the Q source. To hate one's parents and family in the sense of detesting them would be monstrous and not at all characteristic of Jesus. But the Greek word for hate also means to disregard rather than giving preferential treatment to someone. St. Matthew caught the sense of what Jesus was saying when he quotes Jesus as saying: "Whoever loves his father or mother, brother or sister, more than me is not worthy of me." (Mt. 10:37) In other words, Jesus must come first in our lives, first before even those closest to us; he must even be more important to us than our very lives.

Do not fear that you are failing this requirement because your feelings may be very strong toward your family or toward your own life. It's not a matter of feelings of affection, but it's a matter of not letting anyone or anything be valued or become more important than your commitment to Jesus. The martyrs experienced this in giving up their lives rather than turning away from their belief in Jesus. This may sound pretty harsh, but basically it is not much different than the first of the ten Commandments: "I am the Lord thy God, thou shalt not have strange gods before me." Anything in our lives that we would place higher than God, we have made into a god.

The second requirement for discipleship is about carrying our cross and following Jesus. It is similar to the first requirement in that Jesus requires our willingness to face radical self-denial. We have heard this statement before both from Matthew, (10:38) and Mark, (8:35). Thus it probably comes from Mark. The third requirement, a willingness to give up one's material possessions is found only in Luke. (Matthew and Luke seem to have had sources that each could draw from that the other did not). Jesus did not ask everyone he knew to give up all their possessions; some of his friends had to have been well off, but if our possessions prevent us from being able to serve God, then we have to say "goodbye" to them. In Mark 8:36 we do find a similar idea where Jesus says: "What profit is there for one to gain the whole world and forfeit his life (meaning eternal life)? Entering into the Kingdom of God is worth more than all the riches in the world.

Jesus' two little parables, about the tower and about the king going to war, remind us that following Jesus is a serious decision. It is ironic that this example of a king deliberating about going into battle falls on this weekend. Our president is at this moment deliberating over taking military action against Syria. I hope the Holy Spirit guides our legislators in the right direction. This is certainly worthy of our prayers. Amen.

24th Sunday in Ordinary Time
September 15, 2013

INTRODUCTION – (Exodus 32:7-11, 13-14; 1 Timothy 1:12-17; Luke 15:1-32) God's forgiveness is today's theme. Our first reading takes us back to Moses, about 1300 years before Christ. The people of Israel had just escaped from Egypt and were going through the desert of Sinai on their way to the Promised Land. They had already made a covenant with God at Mt. Sinai, and they had promised they would worship only the God of Israel as their God. When God called Moses back to the top of Mt. Sinai to speak with him again, the people got into trouble. They fashioned for themselves a golden calf and worshipped it as their god. This is where our first reading begins. God is angry with his people. Notice, in speaking to Moses, he calls them "your people." Moses intercedes for the people and "convinces" God to be forgiving. His prayer displays total unselfishness. God, of course, forgives them. In the second reading, we hear St. Paul describe what a sinful person he once was and how God was merciful to him. In today's gospel, which is the entire fifteenth chapter of St. Luke, we hear three beautiful parables on God's forgiveness.

HOMILY – We just heard several beautiful stories about God and about God's mercy: the first reading tells us how God forgave his people for worshipping a Canaanite god right after they promised to worship only the God of Israel. We heard how God forgave Paul after he had been persecuting Christians. We heard three parables from Jesus, each one illustrating God's mercy. The readings were long and the message was clear, so I don't think I need to speak very long today. There are just a couple of details I would like to point out. First notice the joy Jesus talks about in each parable. In the story of the prodigal son, the word joy is not used, but we can see the joy expressed by the father when he sees his wayward son. The father runs to him. In that culture older men did not run, it was undignified, but the father ran and welcomed his son, even without giving the son a chance to make his apology. God's happiness is so great when we have been away from him and then we return.

Another detail I want to stress. In the first two parables about the lost sheep and the lost coin, the persons who lost them, the shepherd and the lady, actively searched for what they lost until they found what they were seeking. With the prodigal son, the father did not actively chase after his son to drag him home. He waited and watched and hoped his son might return. As in the parable of the sheep and the coin, God actively seeks to lead us back to himself if we have strayed, but as in the prodigal son, God waits for us to make the decision to return. God respects our free will, and if we choose to separate ourselves from him, it's up to us to choose to return or as the parable puts it, "to come to our senses."

The last thing I want to mention is the older brother. Jesus leaves us in suspense as to whether he forgave his younger brother. We can't be too hard on the older brother for feeling the way he did. Remember, the younger brother asked for his half of the inheritance so everything that was left would eventually belong to the older brother. Here is the forgiving father spending a significant portion of the older brother's assets in order to welcome back his prodigal son. When Jesus tells us "be merciful, just as also your Father is merciful," (Lk. 6:36) it is sometimes a big order. Amen.

25th Sunday in Ordinary Time
September 19, 2010

INTRODUCTION – (Amos 8:4-7; 1 Timothy 2:1-8; Luke 16:1-13) Seven hundred fifty years Before Christ, Israel was enjoying a time of great financial and material prosperity. But spiritually they were bankrupt. In their prosperity they lost their focus on God. The Sabbath and the new moon were days of both prayer and rest. The Israelites resented this interruption in what they considered most important in life – making money. The ephah and shekel, mentioned in our first reading, were weights used in buying and selling. They didn't use honest weights, thereby cheating both their suppliers and their customers. They even exploited their customers by mixing useless materials in with the products they wanted to sell – such as mixing chaff with the wheat. The world has changed considerably since then, but in many ways human nature seems to remain the same.

HOMILY – Late one night, a robber wearing a ski mask jumped into the path of a well-dressed man, stuck a gun in his side and demanded "Give me your money." Indignant, the affluent looking man said, "You can't do this. I'm a United States Congressman!" "In that case," replied the robber, "give me my money."

That's what the rich man in today's gospel wanted: his money. He had heard that his employee was taking advantage of him. Whether the employee was stealing from the rich man or not isn't the main point, although he probably was. And whether the employee reducing the debt that various business people owed his master was honest or dishonest is not the point of the parable either. The main point is that the employee was clever and wasted no time in planning for a secure future for himself.

Jesus tells us we need to be just as clever in planning for a secure future for ourselves, and it's not just for the few years we spend on this earth that we have to provide, but also for our time in eternity. Jesus is constantly reminding us that material things can make us feel so secure in this life that we forget about what is most important, our eternal life. That was the point of today's first reading from Amos. The prosperous era that the Israelites were enjoying 750 years before Christ led them to forget about the God who had blessed them so richly. When they lost touch with God, this led to the moral decline of the nation and its eventual collapse. Our life in this world is temporary. Eternity is forever. Jesus is telling us today to use the blessings God has given us to help us get closer to God and not let our possessions become a god in themselves.

26th Sunday in Ordinary Time
September 29, 2013

INTRODUCTION – (Amos 6:1a, 4-7; 1 Timothy 6:11-16; Luke 16:19-31) Today in our first reading we listen to the prophet Amos. His words are directed to those living in the southern kingdom of Israel – the area we call Judea. He addresses them as "the complacent in Zion." (Zion is another name for Jerusalem). Perhaps this warning came after the Assyrians destroyed the northern kingdom of Israel in 722 BC. The northern kingdom is called Joseph in today's reading, because it was there that their ancestors, descendants of the patriarch Joseph, settled in that area 500 years earlier. The complacent in Jerusalem were living pampered, comfortable lives, paying no attention to the devastation of the north and not concerned that their own country was headed toward the same fate because of their social and moral depravity.

HOMILY – I do not remember anywhere in the Scriptures where Jesus condemned the wealthy simply for having wealth. But he gave many warnings about the dangers of being wealthy. He condemned those who allowed their wealth to make them forget about the God who had blessed them so generously – like the farmer we heard about several weeks ago. He had such a great harvest that he had to tear down his barns to build bigger ones and he gave no thought to the afterlife. Or Jesus condemned those who allowed their wealth to lead them into dishonesty like the unjust steward we heard about last week. Or Jesus condemned those who allowed wealth to make them selfish and self-centered like the rich man in today's gospel.

Today's parable would have been quite a shock for those who heard it. For in Jewish mentality, if a person was wealthy they were assumed to be good people whom God favored. If a person were poor or sick or infirmed, they were assumed to be sinners whom God was punishing for something. But the rich man in today's gospel was not necessarily a virtuous man, his only care in life was caring about himself. And poor Lazarus was not necessarily a sinner – he was just a guy down on his luck. It is a story that reminds us that those who wish to be part of God's kingdom must love God and others. Just as it is the supreme law in a successful marriage, love is the supreme law. The love that Jesus talks about is not necessarily a love based on emotion or feeling good, it flows from a desire to serve and to help others.

What should the rich man have done? Jesus doesn't give us a specific answer. Perhaps in today's parable, Jesus wants us to ask ourselves what we might have done if we were in his place. Does Jesus want us to help everyone we know who is in need? Our world is a lot more complicated than was the world of Jesus. When there is a crisis or disaster on the other side of the world, we know about it instantly. Are we supposed to respond to every appeal for help? It's impossible for any one of us to respond to every need. But because we can't respond to every request for help, does not mean we don't have to respond to any request for help. We have to evaluate what our time and resources allow, what kind of need the other person might have, how real their need is or whether the request is a scam and what responsibility I may have toward them. Charity should begin at home, but it doesn't need to stay there. What does Jesus ask of us? He gives us a hint: we have the Scriptures to guide us – we don't need one of the saints to appear to us to tell us what to do and how we should help others – as Abraham tells the rich man: "they have Moses and the Prophets." If we don't pay attention to the Scriptures, we're not going to be impressed by the appearance of someone who rises from the dead. We come to the Eucharist today to remember where our blessings come from and to offer thanks, and we ask God's help for the days ahead because we never know when we might find that we ourselves are in desperate need of help from others. Amen.

27th Sunday in Ordinary Time
October 6, 2013

INTRODUCTION – (Habakkuk 1:2-3, 2:2-4; 2 Timothy 1:6-8, 13-14; Luke 17:5-10) Six hundred years before Christ, the Babylonians were the dominant power in the Middle East with their capital very near modern day Baghdad. The king of Babylon sought to conquer all the nations that lived in the Middle East, including Israel. For 17 years the Babylonians harassed Israel until they eventually destroyed the Temple and all of Jerusalem. The prophet Habakkuk, who speaks to us in today's first reading, lived during this very difficult period. Habakkuk asks God for relief. God assures him it will come if the people just put their trust in God. However, they didn't. Everything they did under the leadership of the king in Jerusalem was the exact opposite of what God told them to do. So they spent 50 years in exile in Babylon.

HOMILY – Jesus is on his way to Jerusalem. He knew what he would face when he got there. But he had to be faithful to the mission his Father gave him, to preach and heal, to forgive sin and to cast out demons. In today's gospel, we hear about two isolated issues that came up as he and his Apostles journeyed. I will deal with each of these two topics in turn. The first was about faith. The Apostles wanted Jesus to increase their faith. Perhaps they recognized that the jobs that Jesus was giving them required more faith than they had. Jesus seems to have recognized that too, for he told them if they had as much faith as a grain of mustard seed, one of the tiniest of all seeds, they would have more than enough faith to do whatever they needed to do. We can read into Jesus' answer that apparently they didn't have even that much faith. When they asked for more faith,

Jesus didn't just reach into his pocket and pull out a neatly wrapped package of faith for each one of them. Faith is not something one can buy in a store or order over the Internet. It comes through quiet prayer, through the Sacraments, especially the Eucharist, through hearing the word of God and letting it penetrate our minds and hearts and through good works. For example, when we make Mass and Communion an important part of our spiritual life, our faith will grow; when it's something we easily forget about because something more interesting came along to occupy our time, then we will find our faith in Jesus growing weaker. If we want to grow in faith, one very important area to be careful about is the kind of things we say to ourselves. If we say God doesn't hear me, God doesn't care about me, God is too busy for me, we are already doing damage to our faith. If we say to ourselves, I trust that God loves me, I trust God will answer me in some way, I trust that God will not let me down, we are making our faith strong. When the apostles asked for an increase in faith, Jesus couldn't just make it happen because they had things they had to do in their own lives that would cause their faith to strengthen and to grow.

The second part of today's gospel touches on expectations most of us have about God and about how God treats us. God did promise us great rewards if we follow him faithfully, but sometimes we expect those rewards to come more quickly or more abundantly than they seem to and we feel as if God is not being fair. We feel as if we are doing everything we can to please him, but he is not responding to some of the needs we have. Like Habakkuk says in today's reading,

"How long, O Lord, I cry for help but you do not listen." St. Teresa, in a moment of frustration with God said to God one time: "when you treat your friends the way you do, Lord, it's no wonder you have so few of them." In today's gospel passage, Jesus illustrates his point using the example of slavery. It's not that he was approving slavery, it was just a common thing at that time and it served to illustrate what he wanted to say. Jesus tells us if someone was wealthy enough to own a slave or two, they simply told their slave what they wanted done and expected it to be done. They didn't have to praise or thank the slave for whatever the slave did. After all, the slave was someone's property and the slave simply did what he or she was told. God fully owns us and if God did not give us life and sustain us, we would be nothing. He doesn't treat us like a piece of property, however, although he has every right too. He chooses to treat us as his children, he loves us and he will bless us. Jesus died for us and he will reward our faithfulness to himself more abundantly that we can imagine; but he still is in control of the blessings and rewards he has for us. This is what our attitude must be as we try to follow him and obey him: that he's in charge, not you and not me. Or as Jesus put it in the Garden of Gethsemane, "not my will, but thine be done."

Yesterday/Friday was the feast of St. Francis of Assisi. One day in prayer, Francis heard Jesus speaking to him: "Francis, rebuild my house for it is nearly falling down." What did Francis do? Did he go out and start recruiting hundreds of followers who would live a life of poverty, chastity and obedience, write a rule for them and form them into a religious order? No – he did nothing like that! Jesus said: "rebuild my church," so he found churches and chapels in his vicinity that had deteriorated. He replaced bricks that had fallen from the walls of the church and he begged money to buy any materials he needed to do the job right. That is a perfect example of simplicity, humility and obedience of this holy man. He was happy doing what God wanted him to do and he would have been content to do that for the rest of his life. God eventually showed him that rebuilding the Church involved a little more than replacing fallen bricks and stones.

All God wants us to do is to follow him with faith and love. If we do that, God is pleased. He may not always show us his favor or reward us immediately with great blessings. We just need to be satisfied in knowing "we have done what we were obliged to do." Amen.

28th Sunday in Ordinary Time
October 13, 2013

INTRODUCTION – (2 Kings 5:14-17; 2 Timothy 2: 8-13; Luke 17:11-19) Israel and Syria (which is north of Israel and Jordan) have been fighting with each other for centuries. Today's first reading takes us back to 850 BC. They were at war then. At that time Syria was called Aram. Our reading is about an Aramean army general named Naaman. He had the dreaded disease of leprosy. His wife had an Israelite girl who was her slave. This slave was most probably captured in battle. She told her master, Naaman, about a prophet in Israel who would be able to cure his disease. That prophet was Elisha. It must have taken a lot of humility and faith for this proud Aramean general to go into enemy territory (Israel) to look for Elisha. When he located him, Elisha wouldn't even give Naaman the courtesy of coming out of his cave or hut to meet with him. He just told him, through a messenger, to go and bathe in the Jordan River seven times. This, too, was offensive as Naaman considered the rivers in his own country far superior to the Jordan. Naaman was insulted and decided to go back home, but his friends persuaded him to do as the prophet said. Thus our first reading begins. The reading prepares us for the gospel when we hear about Jesus healing 10 people who had leprosy.

HOMILY – St. Paul, in his letter to the Corinthians, asked a very profound question: "What do you have that you have not received?" (1 Cor 4:7) We might want to answer, I've worked hard for what I have. That may be true, but where did you get the energy, the intelligence, the motivation, the skills to be able to accomplish what you did in life? A lot had to be given to us to start with before we could start doing anything on our own. Life itself and everything that came with it is a gift given to us even before we were consulted on the matter.

I know none of us have everything we want, and that's one reason why we are here – to ask God for the things we need. At the same time, we all have been abundantly blessed by having been given so many things that we never even needed to ask for. For those things, we need to give thanks. That is another reason why we are here today – to give thanks.

Luke is the only gospel that tells us about Jesus healing the 10 lepers. The one person who came back to give thanks is so characteristic of our own culture today. Most of us are grateful when God answers a prayer, but how many go out of their way to express that thanks. That is one of the main purposes of the Eucharist, so much so, that the word Eucharist comes from a Greek word with means "Thanksgiving."

Yesterday Joe Webb from Channel 12 came here to St. Boniface and interviewed a few of us so as to do a piece on our porch tour and our 150th anniversary. One of the questions he asked was "what is significant about 150 years of our existence?" That question kept coming back to me the rest of the day. One of the things that is significant about our 150 years is that it showed the dedication the people of this community have toward their faith and toward their parish. Our anniversary has also shown the enduring love God has for his people in this area. Many of my own relatives on my mother's side grew up here, worshipped here, went to school here, were baptized here, married here and were buried here. This loving relationship that has continued for 150 years between God and his people and the support that God's people have shown to this parish is indeed significant. We are celebrating our thankfulness.

One last idea about expressing our thankfulness. Thanksgiving is the key to joy. A person who goes through life with an ungrateful attitude, feeling as if life has been unfair toward them and that life owes them much more than they have received, that person will be a pretty unhappy person. It's the person who knows that God has blessed them, and who has learned to be grateful is the person who is able to be joyful.

All ten people in today's gospel were healed physically. Nine of them went on their way. One of them, however, was touched at a much deeper level in his being and he was converted to Christ and returned to the source of the blessing he received. As we are doing today, he came to Jesus and knelt before the feet of the one who made him whole. Amen

29th Sunday in Ordinary Time
October 20, 2013

INTRODUCTION – (Exodus 17:8-13; 2 Timothy 3:14 - 4:2; Luke 18:1-8) As Moses led God's people from slavery in Egypt, through the desert, to the Promised

Land, they encountered numerous threats to their lives: the army of Pharaoh, the Reed Sea they had to cross, the lack of water and food in the desert. One such threat was opposition from those peoples whose lands they had to pass through to get where they were going. Today's reading speaks of an attack by Amalek, a desert tribe living south of the Dead Sea. Moses positioned himself on a nearby hill to pray for success in battle. He prayed with his arms held high in petition. As long as he prayed, his prayer was powerful and effective. This story is an encouragement to us to persevere in our prayer, which is also the lesson in today's gospel.

HOMILY – Sometimes life doesn't make much sense. Bad things happen, globally, nationally or personally and we wonder why. Is God paying attention, is he too busy to handle all the problems that arise, does he even care? The first book of the Bible, the Book of Genesis, tells us that at the beginning of creation God created a good world and blessed his human creatures with every blessing. But Satan entered the scene and persuaded the first humans to rebel against God. There is so much evil and suffering in the world because we keep following in the footsteps of our ancestors – thinking we're smarter than God and we don't need to do what he tells us. Indeed in ignoring God, we bring many of our problems on ourselves. We also find that even when we do everything God wants us to do, things do not always work out well. Jesus is the perfect example of that; he lived a perfect life and he was condemned as a criminal and nailed to a cross. When bad things happen, especially to good people, we ask "what kind of a God do we have?" Many people have concluded there is no God or, if there is, he doesn't care about me. Their image of God is that God must be like the unjust judge in today's parable: God is unfair and uncaring.

Jesus came to tell us: "No, that's not the way God is." God is caring, God is loving, God hears us and God will answer us. The one problem is that God doesn't always answer us in the way we would like or as quickly as we would like. Contrasting God with the unjust judge, Jesus said at the end of his parable: God "will see to it that justice is done for (his chosen ones) speedily." God views time differently than we do. We want God to see things our way, rather than our being willing to see things his way. Here is where faith comes in, because faith is the willingness to see things his way, the way he has revealed himself to us in Jesus. This is what faith is, to view things as God views them, and because we cannot see everything as clearly as God does, we take God's word for why things are the way they are.

One thing God didn't tell us is why we need to keep on asking for what we need. Jesus tells us we should pray like this poor widow and not stop praying. I remember when I was young, if I asked my parents for something and they said "no," I'd better not ask again. Jesus is telling us to keep on asking. Surely God knows what we need, surely God is not going to forget when we ask for something – remember Jesus told us all the hairs on our head are numbered – he knows every little detail about us. Spiritual writers have given many answers to this question of why we are to keep on asking. They all agree we don't need to keep on asking to keep God informed, but that somehow we need to keep on praying because we are changed thru prayer. We discover more fully our dependence on God as our provider and father; we discover that maybe God has better plans for us; we discover God's providential care and love. For whatever reason, prayer develops our relationship with God and changes us; it does not change God.

Jesus asks at the end of today's gospel: "when the Son

of Man comes, will he find faith on earth?" The answer of course is "yes" he will find faith in those who haven't given up praying – for faith will always be found in those who pray and vice versa. Amen.

30th Sunday in Ordinary Time
October 27, 2013

HOMILY – (Sirach 35:12-14, 16-18; 2 Timothy 4:6-8, 16-18; Luke 18:9-14) Pharisees were lay people who dedicated themselves to trying to keep God's law as perfectly as they could. St. Paul was a Pharisee and Jesus had some followers from among the Pharisee party. They held various theological viewpoints in opposition to the Sadducees (who were the priestly class). Although the gospels tell us a great deal about the opposition between Jesus and the Pharisees, it is interesting to note that it was not so much the Pharisees who fought to have Jesus put to death, it was the Sadducees. The prayer of the Pharisee we hear in today's gospel would have been very characteristic of the prayer of any Pharisee and most probably what the Pharisee said about himself was true. He would have been strict about keeping the law, he would have performed spiritual practices over and above what the law demanded and he would have looked down upon anyone who failed to live up to his standards.

Then there is the publican, a public employee: he worked for the government – the hated Roman government which held Israel in its power and required that taxes be sent annually to Rome. This publican was Jewish, as all of them were, and he was a tax collector. Such individuals were seen as traitors to their own people, and they were seen as thieves as well because this was how they made their living. They collected what would have been the Roman tax, and they added to this tax an additional tax which was their salary. Often the publicans paid themselves well by collecting enough money for a relatively comfortable life style.

In today's gospel, we hear of two men, a publican and a Pharisee who went up to the Temple to pray. The Pharisee was thinking God must have been very proud of him. He was quite proud of himself. The publican realized he didn't have much to be proud of – he simply asked for God's mercy.

I would suspect 98% of us here today are puzzled by this parable. Like the Pharisee most of us can probably say: "I feel as if I'm a pretty good person, I try to keep the Commandments, I try to help my neighbor, I even say the rosary occasionally, I drop my collection envelope in the basket every week or every month. I'm glad I'm not like a lot of other people I know." After the Pharisee listed all his good qualities, Jesus tells us he did not get right with God. So where did he go wrong? All the things he did were good things, except maybe for his thinking he was better than most everyone else. He forgot one important element in the spiritual life. It begins with humility. It begins with knowing that God is the source of our justification. It begins with the awareness that it is God who saves us. As a Pharisee, St. Paul, who for a time thought himself superior to those who believed in Christ, tells us later in his life in his Letter to the Romans: "All have sinned and fall short of the glory of God." (Rom. 3:23) Two chapters later he emphasizes it: "Death spread to all humans because all people sinned." (Rom. 5:12) None of us escape the guilt of sin and being humble enough to admit that and to ask God's mercy is the first and most important step to be right with God. That's where the Pharisee in today's parable got off the right track, he was full of pride at his own self-righteousness rather than being grateful for the righteousness of God. I wonder if those who have given up going to Mass have lost this awareness that our holiness and justification begins with a humble recognition of our need for God's mercy. You might notice that's the way Mass begins. By acknowledging we are not perfect when we approach God, we approach him in need of God's mercy.

Does all this mean we do not need to worry about keeping the Commandments or doing good works. Jesus stresses how important that is in so many passages in the Scriptures, but today, the gospel tells us how we are to begin our approach to God.

Do you wonder if there is any hope for the Pharisee who tried to serve God with such fidelity all his life. Certainly! There is always the hope that he would eventually look deep into his own heart and realize how self-centered, pompous, judgmental and ungrateful he was in life. Maybe then he would do more than say thank you God that I'm better than everyone else. He might recognize that he is like everyone else, in need of God's saving love and grace for only Jesus is our Savior.

31st Sunday in Ordinary Time
November 3, 2013

HOMILY – (Wisdom 11:22-12:2; 2 Thessalonians 1:11-2:2; Luke 19:1-10) A young family went to a nice restaurant for dinner one evening. One of the little boys in the family happened to find a bright shiny dime and was fascinated by it. He put it in his mouth and started to choke on it. The parents became frantic and started calling for anyone to help their choking son. A man at a nearby table came over, turned the boy upside down, gave him a few swats and the dime came out. The parents were so grateful and asked the man "are you a doctor or a medical practitioner?" No the man said, I work for the IRS.

Diocesan policy requires pastors to present the parish finance report to the parish at or near the end of the fiscal year. Well the fiscal year ended on June 30, but with my vacation and knee replacement and other events, this turned out to be the most convenient Sunday for me to present it to you. I always like to choose a Sunday where the readings have something to do with money so my homily doesn't stray too far from the theme of the gospel. Today's gospel has a lot to do with money. Last week we heard about two people who went up to the Temple to pray. One was a Pharisee and one was a Publican. You might recall, I described the publican as a public employee who was basically a tax collector. He collected taxes from his fellow Jews to give to the Romans who ruled over the entire Middle East. Also I explained that when tax collectors collected taxes, they always included something for themselves (determined at their discretion) which provided the tax collector and his family a means of support. Some were very generous toward themselves when they added on the additional tax. Rome didn't care how much they added on as long as Rome got the amount they thought should come to them. Today we hear about a chief tax collector who made quite a comfortable living at his job. But when he met Jesus, his life changed as it has changed for so many. Honesty and concern for the poor and needy replaced cheating and greed as the dominant driving force in his life. That day salvation came to his house.

When I look at our own finance statement, I have to look at it with a considerable amount of appreciation for what our parishioners do for St. Boniface Church. A couple of years ago we had a drive to increase offerings and it was very successful. It seems to me that this past fiscal year people have continued to donate the amount they had originally pledged. We did end fiscal year 2012-2013 in the red, having $6100 more in expenses than we had in income, but considering that we had large expenses for renovating the Church, we did quite well. And none of the expenses we had for our renovation had to be paid for out of our savings. That figure of $6100 represents less than 1% of the entire budget. All this says I am grateful we did so well.

Remember, however, that these are figures from last June. Some of you may have noticed that our Sunday collections recently have been quite a bit less than what we need to meet our expenses. I know that some people are having a difficult time financially. I know that our Sunday attendance has been going down and our population is getting older. This year in October our count was just under 400 people coming weekly to Sunday Mass. That is a drop of 8% from last year. Some people have suggested that we lost people during the renovation while the scaffolds were up, or the floor was torn up, or whatever and they never came back afterwards. But all is not lost. New condos and homes are being built in the neighborhood and, hopefully, some percent of those homes will be occupied by Church-going Catholics who have not yet discovered where we are. I hope they discover us soon because at the rate we are going, we are going to end the fiscal year $30,000 in the red. That is not so good.

We have to do something or in a few years we will go broke. I am suggesting that everyone increase their weekly donation by about $3 or $4 dollars a week. I suspect you will never miss it and I'm sure it will come back to you in some form or another. The Lord is not going to let any of us outdo him in generosity. I've always experienced that. If you can do better, it will be very helpful, because not everyone will be able to make an increase of any kind. I want to end on two positive thoughts, the renovation for the church has been paid for and the church should remain in good condition for quite a few years now (barring any unforeseen catastrophe). Secondly, when we have our big celebration of our anniversary in the spring, that celebration has been paid for by a generous donor. The cost for the celebration is not coming from your Sunday contribution.

I am well aware that most of the people who come to St. Boniface are folks who live outside of Northside. I am also aware that many of our parishioners are very generous. I am often amazed at how generous some people are. I just want to thank you for coming to St. Boniface and thank you for helping to keep us in the business of serving God and serving God's people. Amen.

All Saints
November 1, 2013

INTRODUCTION – (Rev. 7:2-4, 9-14; 1 John 3:1-3; Mt. 5:1-12a) In its four and a half billion years, our planet has seen an overwhelming number of catastrophes, earthquakes, volcanoes, hurricanes, collisions with meteors, ice ages, plagues, etc. Somehow, under God's creative hand, planet earth continues to survive while life on this earth not only survives but thrives greatly. We not only have natural catastrophes to be concerned about, but we humans, through our brilliance, have discovered ways to annihilate all of creation if we are not wise and prudent. Will our planet, and life on this planet, continue to survive the many disasters that could come our way, forever? The Book of Revelation, right before the passage we will hear today, is a description of the end of the world and it asks a critical question: "who can survive?"

The answer to that question is not all doom and gloom but a message of hope. The answer is described in today's first reading: Those who have followed Christ faithfully will survive. They will be identified and marked as faithful followers of Christ. As such they will receive his special protection during that time when the end of the world is to come. The first group of those who are to be marked and saved from the ordeal that is to come are from among the Jews: 144,000. It is a symbolic number representing completeness – 12,000 from each of the 12 tribes. The following vision is a vision of all of Christ's followers, a number that was impossible to count because there were so many. Along with the Jews who came to believe in Christ, they will share in Christ's victory over death and enjoy the blessing of eternal happiness forever.

HOMILY – From the earliest days of the Church, believers always had deep respect for those who willingly gave their lives for Christ. And many did. They were called martyrs, a word that means witnesses, for when the Roman emperors started persecuting Christians and tried to get them to give up their faith, the martyrs witnessed to Jesus by choosing to die rather than turning away from Jesus. The first martyr was St. Steven. Most of the apostles were martyred. Three hundred years after Jesus ascended, the Holy Father established a feast for all the martyrs, to be celebrated every year, so we don't forget the heroism of these holy men and women. Two centuries later there were too many martyrs as well as too many holy men and women whom the Church wanted to honor that there were not enough days in the year to honor each one individually. So the Holy Father made that feast a feast for all saints, men and women whose lives were examples of holiness for all of us, whether they were martyrs or not.

Three months ago, before my knee operation, my friend and classmate, Fr. Jerry Bensman went on vacation. It was an interesting vacation in that we visited places neither of us had ever seen, Yellowstone National Park with all its geysers and buffalo and elk in Wyoming. We drove on to the majestic high mountains of the Grand Tetons, then on to Salt Lake City and ultimately to Aspen and then to Denver, Colorado. Often I wondered how we would have found all these places without maps and GPS. There were various roads we could have taken, but without the map showing us the right roads, we would never have gotten where we wanted to go. I think of the saints somewhat that way. Through their holy lives, they have shown us the way to serve God and to be with God forever. Their lives were different in many ways, some lived for a long time, some died young, some lived active lives, some lived quiet lives of prayer, some were brilliant, some were just average, some were married and had children, some lived a single life, some were great sinners, some lived devout lives most of their lives. But like the many roads that would take us where we wanted to go on vacation, the lives of the saints may have followed different routes – some such as dedicating their life to prayer, some by dedicating their life to helping the poor or the sick, some by dedicating their life to teaching, etc., but they all led to the same place: loving God and loving others.

Their lives give us an example of how to live, and we need that example for without it we may be trying to make a long trip without a map. Where they have gone, we hope to be with them some day, with God and with each other in God's kingdom. Someday, hopefully, we will be part of that countless group of people in heaven, for being a saint is the vocation each of us has. Amen.

All Souls
November 2, 2008

INTRODUCTION – (2 Maccabees 12:43-46: Romans 5:5-11, John 6:37-40) Our first reading, from the book of Maccabees, comes from about 100 years before Christ. At that time in history the Greeks were the dominant power and they were trying to get the Jews to abandon their faith and follow the beliefs of the pagans. Those who would not give in were persecuted and put to death. The loyal Jews fought back. In one of their battles, many Jews were killed. As they were being buried, it was found that they had small statues of pagan gods attached to their garments. These Jews were loyal to their Jewish beliefs, but they had, to some extent, given in to paganism. Just in case those pagan gods were real, they were carrying with them statues of pagan gods to give them protection. Their leader, Judas Maccabeus, took up a collection to send to Jerusalem for sacrifices to be offered up to the Lord for those people. He believed their hearts were, in general, in the right place, but for the weakness in their faith they had to be forgiven. In this piece of history from 100 B.C., we can see the beginnings of the belief that our prayers can help those who have died, a belief that is still part of our faith.

HOMILY – Praying for our deceased relatives and friends is what our feast of All Souls is about today. However, I had the hardest time getting started with today's homily. I kept putting it off. It's not as if I do not believe in praying for friends and relatives who have died. I do it all the time and it has been a tradition in the Church from the beginning, and even before that as we heard in our first reading. I think the difficulty I had in developing my homily comes from two sources. First, many people don't like to hear about death and what might come afterwards. We know we can't avoid it, but my sense is that many people believe that if they don't think about it, it won't happen, at least not for a long time. My suspicion is that my father was that way. I constantly tried to get him to make a will but he never did. As a CPA he would have known it was a good idea. I think making a will would have made the prospect of his own death too concrete and too real for him to deal with. The second reason today's homily was hard was that I would have to talk about Purgatory. It's an idea that many Christians deny. I remember once I was helping a family prepare the liturgy for their deceased father and they insisted "absolutely no mention of Purgatory." It's as if it were a bad word. They wanted to think their father was perfect, I guess, and was already in heaven. Most of us would like to believe that our loved ones go straight to heaven when they die – period. If this were true, then they would not need our prayers. If they went to the other place, God forbid, our prayers would do them no good. The Church teaches, in every Mass we have for a person who died and in today's feast, that our prayers do help our relatives and friends who have left this world as they journey to eternal life.

Purgatory, among all the mysteries and beliefs of the Church is an extremely logical and comforting doctrine. It's logical if we ask ourselves how many of us think we will be perfect when we die. There may even be some who are perfect right now. I would ask them to identify themselves, but if they're perfect, they will also be too humble to do so. Even those who lived a good life may still have a little room for improvement, they may still not love God or others quite enough. That's where Purgatory comes in – it's an opportunity to grow into the most loving, most holy person we can possibly be. As a result we would then be filled with God's peace and joy and love to the fullest extent. Luther rejected the idea of Purgatory because of the abuse of indulgences at the time. Today, the concept of Purgatory has been rejected by many because of all the negative images of suffering and punishment that we grew up with. Actually, I think for the souls in Purgatory, happiness far outweighs the unhappiness. Their salvation is sure, they are more closely united with God than they had ever experienced before in their lives, they are on their way to the enjoyment of God's kingdom in the fullest possible way. But they're not there yet and that's the painful part.

If you read the book, "The Five People You Meet in Heaven," I think you get a good, practical image of Purgatory. It's not a religious book, it's very entertaining and it pictured for me what Purgatory might be like as we work out issues, regrets, hurts, conflicts, etc., that we might take with us when we die. To demonstrate that Purgatory makes so much sense, I think that those who deny Purgatory have had to find a substitute for it in their thinking about the next life. For many that substitute is reincarnation. In reincarnation a person supposedly keeps working for greater and greater purity and holiness until they are ready to be perfectly one with God. However, reincarnation comes from Hinduism. Actually a Hindu does not look forward to reincarnation because they don't want to have to pass through this world of pain and suffering one more time. I suspect the notion of reincarnation has been adopted by many Westerners, even Christians, because it fits our culture of "buy now, pay later." They figure they can live any way they want and can postpone having to pay any consequences. Our faith tells us, "now is the acceptable time, now is the day of salvation." God gives us what we need in this life to help us know him and serve him in this life. If we do not do it perfectly, Purgatory is there to finish the job. Today, we renew our faith in life after death. Today too we renew our belief in the power of prayer to help our loved ones, even those who are no longer among us, for in Christ they are still one with us. With Christ our great high priest, we offer now the greatest prayer there is, the Eucharist.

32nd Sunday in Ordinary Time
November 10, 2013

INTRODUCTION – (2 Maccabees 7:1-2, 9-14; 2 Thess. 2:16-3, 5; Luke 20:27-38) Alexander the Great conquered every nation from Sicily and Egypt all the way to India. This area included Israel. He did it all in twelve years. In his spare time, when he wasn't busy conquering, he founded 70 cities. Alexander died at the age of 32 in 323 BC! At his death, his empire was divided among three of his generals, who with their successors, ruled for about 250 years until the Romans gained power in the first century. Our first reading today takes us about 150 years after Alexander to 175 BC when an ambitious Greek ruler named Antiochus IV came to power. He decided to create religious unity throughout his kingdom. He thus made it a crime for the Jews to practice their Jewish religion. Circumcision was forbidden. Copies of the Scriptures were burned. Jews could not follow their dietary laws or celebrate their usual feasts. The worship of Greek gods and goddesses was required. Some of the Jews gave in to the Greeks, while others fought hard to hold on to their traditional faith. Our first reading gives us just a hint of how terrible this time was for the Jews who were faithful. If you look for this passage in your bible at home, it describes the torture of seven brothers and their heroic mother. A shorter portion of this reading was chosen today because it reflects that many Jews at that time, 175 years before Christ, believed that all who were faithful to Yahweh in this life would rise to new life in the resurrection on the last day. The passage prepares us for the gospel where the Sadducees challenged Jesus about the resurrection, which was something they did not believe in.

HOMILY – We need to know a little something about the religious politics of Judaism at the time of Jesus in order to make sense of today's gospel. The Sadducees, who feature in today's gospel, were the archconservatives in Jesus' time. They were connected with the aristocracy and the Jewish priesthood. They did not accept any part of the Bible except the first five books. And they did not believe in angels, spirits and the resurrection of the dead on the last day. What they are trying to do in today's gospel is to prove, with an extreme example, that there can be no resurrection. Their example is based on a law that comes out of the Book of Leviticus (the 3rd book of the Bible which was one they accepted). The law is known as levirate marriage and it stated: if a man died and he had no children, then his brother was supposed to marry the man's widow and through her bring children into the world. Adding another wife to the family would have required quite an adjustment, but it solved some serious problems – such as seeking to preserve the name and memory of the brother who died, keeping in the family whatever property the brother had, and ensuring that the widow would be provided for. The Sadducees really didn't believe there was life after this life, but even if there were, in their minds it would be very similar to life the way we know it now. Jesus tells them that's where they went wrong in their thinking. Jesus said it would be entirely different. We will not die, we will be like angels, we will be children of God and we will rise. This gives us a lot to speculate about (especially what being like angels means), but exactly what any of this means is still a mystery. It will always remain a mystery because we have nothing in this world to use as a comparison for what is to come. I do find it interesting however to read about people who have had near death experiences. It helps one's imagination to visualize the next world just a little better than having nothing at all to help us picture what it might be like.

Sometimes today's gospel causes people to be distressed because they think that once they pass into the next life they lose touch with those they have loved in this life. I think we will still be in touch with those we have been close to in this life. Why should we be separated from those who have supported us and helped us to attain eternal life? One of the common experiences those who have been clinically dead and who have returned to this life report is that most often the first persons they meet in the next life are parents, grandparents, relatives and friends.

Perhaps the most important message the gospel gives us today is to assure us that God has created us for eternal life, a life much more wonderful than anything we can imagine. Remember St. Paul's statement: "eye has not seen nor ear heard nor has it entered into our hearts what things God has prepared for those who love him." So in bad times, we must remember there are better times ahead. In good times, we cannot forget about the even greater happiness God has prepared for those who love him and are faithful to him.

33rd Sunday in Ordinary Time
November 17, 2013

INTRODUCTION – (Malachi 3:19-20a; 2 Thess. 3:7-12; Luke 21:5-19) In our first reading today, we hear from the prophet Malachi who lived about 470 years before Christ. Many Jews at that time were apathetic about their religious duties and about keeping the Commandments. He warns his listeners that the day of reward and punishment is coming. He uses fire as a symbol to represent both the reward and the punishment. It will be scorching heat for those who have not followed God's ways and will bring warmth and healing to those who have been faithful.

HOMILY – A priest, who had just arrived in heaven, was being taken to his eternal dwelling. It was only a small shack and the priest couldn't hide his disappointment. Down the street he saw a taxi driver being shown a lovely estate with gardens and pools. "I don't understand it," the priest said. "My whole life, I served God with everything I had and this is all I get, while this cabbie is given a mansion?" "It's quite simple," St. Peter said. "When you preached, people slept; when he drove, people prayed." (from *Laughter, the Best Medicine, Reader's Digest,* pg 342)

We'll try not to let that happen today. One commentator, Fr. Joseph Fitzmeyer, a Scripture scholar at the Catholic University of America, wrote that this section of the gospel is one of the most difficult parts of the gospel to interpret. "There are as many interpretations of it as there are heads that think about it." (*the Anchor Bible, the Gospel According to Luke,* pg. 1323) Fr. Fitzmeyer, in this statement, is referring to practically the whole of chapter 21, verses 5 to 38. That whole section of Luke is often called Jesus' "eschatological discourse" because it deals with the eschata, a Greek word that means "last things." It deals with the end of the Jewish Temple, the end of Jerusalem and the end of the world. In the Jewish mind, all of these things were lumped together. For a Jew, how could he or she conceive of a world without the Temple? In the Jewish mind, the end of the Temple would have meant the end of sacrifice, and surely sacrifice would end only with the world itself. (Bruce Vawter, *the Four Gospels*, pg 323) Today's gospel is the first part of this larger section in Luke. As I just said, the "eschatological discourse" is 33 verses long. The passage you just heard me read is 14 verses long. If you want to read the whole section, you will have to get your bibles out when you get home and look up chapter 21 in Luke.

I have a couple of points I want to make regarding this passage regarding the end of the Temple and the end of Jerusalem. St. Luke seems to separate what Jesus said about the destruction of the Temple and the destruction of Jerusalem from the end of the world and the second coming of Christ because when Luke wrote his gospel, the Temple and Jerusalem had already been destroyed. The Romans burnt the city in late August, early September of the year 70 AD and Luke wrote his gospel about 10 or 15 years later.

One interesting fact that I learned in preparing my homily concerns Jesus' warnings not to be misled by people claiming to be the Messiah or claiming to speak in his name. Jesus said do not follow them. In hindsight, we see his warning was very practical. Josephus, the famous Jewish historian, tells us that on the day the Temple was burnt, 6000 people died in the Temple area. They were there because a false prophet announced that God commanded the people to go to the Temple in order to be saved, so 6000 went and perished. Our world is full of false prophets today. We have to be careful that the prophetic voice we follow comes from someone who truly speaks for God.

There are two other points we might remember from today's gospel. In spite of the persecutions Jesus predicted, he predicts victory for those who remained faithful to him. Even in the face of persecution, Jesus could say: "not a hair of your head will be lost. It is by your endurance that you will make your lives secure." It is an assurance of real life, life eternal, for those who remain faithful to Jesus.

Another point is that as we come to the end of the Church year, which will be in two weeks, and as we come to the end of the calendar year in six and a half weeks, we are reminded that all things will eventually come to an end: our life in the present world and eventually all of this material world. One thing only will last, our life with God, a life that begins now in this life and which is nourished through the sacraments, prayer and good works. The most important thing we can do in this life is to never lose the divine life Jesus has offered to share with us. Amen.

Christ the King
November 21, 2010

INTRODUCTION – (2 Samuel 5:1-3; Colossians 1:12-20; Luke 23:35-43) When the first king of Israel, King Saul, was killed in battle, the southern part of Israel (the tribes of Judah) chose David as their king. The northern part chose Ishbaal, King Saul's son, to be their king. Ishbaal was inept and after seven years of chaos, the northern tribes turned to David and asked him to rule them also. This is where our first reading comes in. David was a brilliant and far-sighted military and political leader. David was able to conquer his enemies on all sides. In spite of his serious moral misadventures, for which he repented, the Jews always hoped for another king with his talents and capabilities. Kings were anointed when they assumed office, thus the king was called "the anointed one." The Hebrew word for this is "Mashiah," or as we say it: "Messiah." As time went on, especially after the kingdom was destroyed by the Babylonians, the Jews longed for a king, a descendant of David, an anointed one, who would again rule in Israel and who would establish the peaceful and bountiful reign of God. When Mashiah is translated into Greek we have "Χριστός." ("Christos"). So when we call Jesus "Christ" we are in effect saying Jesus, the anointed one; i.e., the King. Christ's kingdom is not an earthly one, as St. Paul tells us, but it is eternal and a sharing in God's own authority, power and glory.

HOMILY – After the evening meal, with father, mother and little five-year old Brian, mother left the family rather quickly. Brian wanted to know where his mother was going. Dad said, "Mommy is going to a Tupperware party." He thought for a moment, then asked, "What's a Tupperware party?" Dad always tended to give simple, honest answers so he said, "Well, Brian, a Tupperware party is where a bunch of ladies sit around and sell plastic bowls to each other." Brian nodded as if he understood, then burst out laughing and asked, "Come on, Dad, what is it really?" (from *Laughter, the Best Medicine, Reader's Digest,* pg 71)

Brian could not picture a lot of ladies sitting around selling bowls to one another. The Jews, by and large, couldn't picture Jesus as their Messiah and King and they didn't think it was funny when the Apostles preached that he was. The Jews thought they knew what the Messiah was supposed to be: a glorious military and political leader, an idealized kind of King David who would overcome all their enemies, restore the kingship to Israel and initiate a reign of peace and prosperity.

They also knew their Scriptures for they listened to them every week and they knew Deuteronomy 21:23 which said, "God's curse rests on him who hangs on a tree." They could not conceive of Jesus, a convicted criminal, crucified and hanging on a cross, as their Messiah. Pilate might have thought it some kind of a twisted joke that would embarrass the Jewish people to put a sign above Jesus' head, which said he was the King of the Jews. But, by and large, especially among the Jewish leaders, the idea of Jesus as Messiah was not only offensive, but blasphemous, and they were ready to punish anyone who acknowledged that Jesus was their Messiah, their king. Jesus tried to tell them that his kingdom would be different from any kingdom they had ever known: "My kingdom is not of this world." Perhaps some of them could see how different his kingdom would be when they challenged him to save himself and he didn't. They knew of his amazing powers, but he chose not to use them to save himself. Instead he was willing to suffer extraordinary pain and humiliation to save us.

Think for a moment how great a faith the "good thief" had to be able to have to recognize Jesus as a king: "Jesus, remember me when you come into your kingdom." Nowhere in any of the literature of that time do we find anyone who anticipated their Messiah would have to suffer. Their Messiah would be a glorious, powerful figure. The "good thief" had to be able to see through all the expectations of the Jewish people; he had to be able to see through the weakness and failure that he was able to observe in Jesus and to affirm that Jesus was indeed a king. It is an act of faith that each of us must make individually if he is to be our king, and if we wish to be with him in his kingdom, a kingdom that will be for each of us the fullness of life that he came to bring us.

It is interesting that is was only 85 years ago that the Church established this feast of Our Lord, Jesus Christ the King. It was instituted as a corrective to the secular atmosphere of the times. However, as we can see in today's second reading. honoring Jesus as king has been part of the tradition of the Church from the beginning. This passage is "one of the most important theological statements about the person of Christ in the New Testament." (*The Collegeville Bible Commentary*, pg 1182) It proclaims that Christ existed before all creation and is preeminent among all creatures and that all things were created through his mediation. Therefore, he existed before all creation and is preeminent among all creatures. One verse is especially appropriate for this week of Thanksgiving as we read: "Let us give thanks to the Father, who has made you fit to share in the inheritance of the holy ones in light. He delivered us from the power of darkness and brought us into the kingdom of his beloved Son." "Let us give thanks," the letter to the Colossians says, it doesn't suggest we just say thanks. Giving thanks involves more than just saying it.

That brings us to why we are here today, to give thanks for God's many blessings, especially for bringing us into the kingdom of his beloved Son. Being part of his kingdom is an honor and a privilege that, although we do not appreciate it as much as we should now, we will praise God for all of eternity, and we will never grow tired of doing so. So let us give thanks to the Lord our God. Amen.

Rosella Robinson Funeral
November 12, 2005

HOMILY – In Rosella we have all had a good friend. Offering sympathy is in order, because we've lost a stepmother, a grandmother, an aunt, a friend, a wonderful lady. At the same time we are not here to grieve but to celebrate. We celebrate that Rosella lived a good and full life for 95 years, that she died a peaceful death, that she lived and died filled with God's grace. We also celebrate our faith that she is now enjoying the rewards of eternal life. As our first reading says: "The souls of the just are in the hand of God, and no torment shall touch them. They seemed in the view of the foolish to be dead…but they are in peace." For the bible, a fool is someone who doesn't believe in God. Their vision of reality is limited. Their mind is closed to anything they cannot discover for themselves. So death is the end of life in the view of a foolish person, since they have no belief in God. But for one who has faith, there is more to life than just the few years we spend on this earth. There is unending life with God. If a fool is someone who doesn't believe in God, then by those standards, Rosella was a person with profound and extraordinary wisdom. Her life was centered on God and her prayers were for those she loved that they too would live a life centered on God.

I was talking with George the other evening and he said whenever she called him she would introduce herself as: "This is Rosella, your godmother." She took her role seriously. George said by reminding him she was his godmother, he thinks she was also reminding him that she had the responsibility and the authority to straighten him out if he needed it. I'm sure all her godchildren got gentle reminders at times and I'm sure they got lots of extra prayers as well.

The gospel I chose for our Mass today was on the Eucharist. The Eucharist was so important to Rosella. She would come to Mass every day when she could. Jesus tells us "Whoever eats my flesh and drinks my blood has eternal life, and I will raise him on the last day." It is in this faith that I can say we are here to celebrate, knowing Rosella was well nourished with the bread of life, the body and blood of Jesus who promised: "whoever eats this bread will live forever."

In 1952 our mother, Alice, died. Rosella knew Alice and often Rosella told me that because of the friendship they shared, she felt she should step in and help out after Alice died. And she did when she married my father in February, 1953. For over 52 years she has been with us. She was a caregiver through and through. When she was finished caring for us, she cared for her sister, Catherine, and she cared for her grandchildren. It was what made her happy, to be needed by someone. And she didn't want to inconvenience anyone. She would always tell me, "Now if you have something planned and something happens to me, don't change your plans. Just go ahead with what you were going to do."

All kinds of great things could be said about Rosella, her kindness, her gentleness, her faith, her dedication to family. One thing I always remarked about was that I seldom heard her say a negative thing about anyone. Dad would often get frustrated with her when he wanted to complain about someone and she would make excuses for them or stand up for them.

I have no worries about where she is now. I'm sure she can say with St. Paul: "I have fought the good fight, I have finished the race, I have kept the faith. From now on a merited crown awaits me…" I believe she now must have a double crown, the first for living with my father (I loved my father, but those who knew him will understand what I mean). The second crown would be for taking over the care of five children, four in grade school and me in high school.

Since she's been at the Little Sisters, who took wonderful care of her, I would try to visit her every week. Whenever I was about to leave she would say "If I don't see you next week, I'll be on my way to heaven." She was peaceful with her God, with herself and with those who knew her. She was ready to go. So I can't grieve. I can only say thank you God for giving us a good woman to take care of us when we needed her, a good woman to inspire us in the way of holiness and a good woman to pray for us and whom I am sure will continue to pray for us until we're all together.

When she died a week ago we were enjoying the beautiful colors of fall. The red and yellow and gold trees were telling us that summer is over. But we do not grieve that the green leaves are gone and that nature is shutting down for we know it's only temporary. Spring will return and so will a new life for Rosella and for all of us, a life that will never end. Amen.

Fr. Lammeier's Funeral
July 11, 2015

HOMILY – (Isaiah 25:6. 7-9; 1 Thessalonians 4:13-18; John 14:1-6) I would like to begin with a quotation from Fr. Lammeier's will. No! he did not leave instructions to give everyone $1000 who came to his funeral. But he did give instructions about the homily for his Funeral Mass. He wrote in his will this (quote) "request that the homilist talk on 'death' or the priesthood. Please no eulogy. There is not an awful lot of good that can be said, and I would want the homily to be a little longer than that." (unquote)

I would not agree with Fr. Lammeier on that. There is an "awful lot of good that can be said," but I'm not going to say everything that could be said because I may be haunted by Fr. Lammeier some evening for not following his instructions. I hope no one objects to my calling Fr. Lammeier "Zib." It was a nickname his mother gave him when he was small and he told me he doesn't know what it means or why she called him that. I've been calling him Zib for the past 15 years or more when he was helping me at St. Boniface. We were blest by Fr. Lammeier's willingness to help us. He was a very humble man, highly respected, had a good sense of humor, worked hard on his homilies and described himself as a simple priest who said his prayers and did his work. He influenced many people by his wisdom, whether it was one of the two archbishops he served as their administrative secretary, Archbishops Leibold and Bernardin, or whether it was the ordinary parishioner who came to him with a problem or for confession on a Saturday afternoon. He treated everyone with equal dignity and kindness.

For about 18 months, he lived at St. Boniface Church and it was an honor and privilege to have him there. He tried very hard not to inconvenience any of the staff. Often when people visited him, instead of saying "goodbye" he always said "try to be nice." The way he was telling others to live is the way he lived, treating others in a friendly and benevolent way.

This is getting too much like a eulogy, which Zib didn't want. He said to talk about the priesthood or death. Well, I will say something about both. Regarding priesthood, Zib loved being a priest. Saying Mass in the morning was the highlight of his day. The day he died, he had concelebrated Mass with the other priests at St. Margaret Hall. He was faithful to the divine office, the rosary and holy hours at church. He was not a monk or a hermit, he had a well-rounded personality; he enjoyed reading, watching sports on TV and keeping in touch with his many friends.

On the topic of death, Zib died peacefully. It was in a way a blessing because his sciatica had been really causing him a lot of pain. We've heard three scripture readings on death. Isaiah pictures it as something God is going to eliminate at the end of time (he will destroy death forever and wipe away the tears from all faces) and to those who have remained faithful, God will provide a wonderful banquet (and since death and tears – including such things as starvation - will be done away with, the banquet will be unending).

Paul tells us in the second reading about Christ's second coming. The Thessalonians were worried that their friends and family who had already died would miss out on the grand event of Jesus' return at the end of time. Paul said, don't worry, those who have already died will rise first then all of us together will be taken up to meet our Lord, our king, visibly enthroned in glory.

In the gospel Jesus assures us there's plenty of room in God's great kingdom and he will have a place ready for those who follow him. We will be with him always. The words of the gospel we just heard come from the Last Supper, shortly before Jesus' arrest. With the conviction that his followers would be with him always, he tells them "do not let your hearts be troubled." It was easy for Jesus to say, but hard to do for the apostles considering what they were soon going to have to face.

Jesus always says to us during difficult times: "do not let your hearts be troubled." The loss of Zib is sad. He had so many talents and so many good qualities. Now, instead of having the support of his inspiration and encouragement, we have to let go, we have to say goodbye. But it's only a temporary goodbye. As we follow the way, the truth and the life, we will all meet again in the everlasting kingdom of God's love. May our faith be strong and may our hearts not be troubled, and as Zib would say to us if he were to leave us with any words of wisdom: "try to be nice."

From Rita Robinson Ring,
Co-founder of Shepherds of Christ

God has chosen us, we are to turn to Christ with greater generosity, and as baptized Christians to grow in our knowing and loving capacity.

God has put His handprint on us in baptism giving to us the virtues of faith, hope and love. These are theological virtues. We must pray to God for the increase in these virtues and we respond to the grace He outpours to us. In praying for the increase in faith we can see more and more the vision of the Heavenly Father. We can hope for our eternal salvation and help spread that hope in our lives to others and we can share more deeply in God's loving activity – loving more supernaturally as we cooperate by responding to the gifts given by God of greater faith, hope and love.

God is with us, God wants us to spread the good news, to turn toward Him in loving union performing good acts according to His will.

Fr. Joe's book teaches us about love and life in God. Fr. Joe's book teaches us about the gift of the Mass and the Church, and about salvation history. We live more every day according to the scriptures in peace, love and joy. We know Jesus, we love Him. He is operating in us.

We all seek happiness – Happiness is found in God –

In reading the weekly scriptures and reading Fr. Joe's homily – God's loving self-communication to us will grow in our lives – as we respond in love to Him.

This book and the scripture come alive in our lives every Sunday after we read the scriptures and Fr. Joe's homily before Mass.

God communicates His own life through grace and man in return gives himself to God and his fellowman in loving service.

Happiness comes to us in dying to those ways not likened to God and rising in the spiritual life in that image and likeness of Christ.

We love Fr. Joe's jokes that help us to clear our minds and laugh and listen.

He told me of a little boy who was drawing a picture in art class and the teacher said "Who is this?" And the little boy said, "It is God."

The teacher said, "Nobody knows what God looks like." The little boy said, "When I get done – they will know."

In baptism we have been given a sharing in God's life with this elevated knowing and loving capacity.

It is up to us to pray to God for the grace to grow to know and love Him more – to be more and more likened to God.

In the pages of Fr. Joe's homilies we learn more and more about God, about loving God and loving others as ourselves – God is love – God is the source of love – We are to Respond to God's love.

Excerpt from *Response to God's Love* by Fr. Edward Carter, S.J.

"... In reference to Christianity, God himself is the ultimate mystery. Radically, God is completely other and transcendent, hidden from man in his inner life, unless he chooses to reveal himself. Let us briefly look at this inner life of God.

The Father, in a perfect act of self-expression, in a perfect act of knowing, generates his son. The

Son, the Word, is, then, the immanent expression of God's fullness, the reflection of the Father. Likewise, from all eternity, the Father and the Son bring forth the Holy Spirit in a perfect act of loving.

At the destined moment in human history, God's self-expression, the Word, immersed himself into man's world. God's inner self-expression now had also become God's outer self-expression. Consequently, the mystery of God becomes the mystery of Christ. In Christ, God tells us about himself, about his inner life, about his plan of creation and redemption. He tells us how Father, Son, and Holy Spirit desire to dwell within us in the most intimate fashion, how they wish to share with us their own life through grace. All this he has accomplished and does accomplish through Christ. St. Paul tells us: "I became a minister of this Church through the commission God gave me to preach among you his word in its fullness, that mystery hidden from ages and generations past but now revealed to his holy ones. God has willed to make known to them the glory beyond price which this mystery brings to the Gentiles — the mystery of Christ in you, your hope of glory. This is the Christ we proclaim while we admonish all men and teach them in the full measure of wisdom, hoping to make every man complete in Christ" (Col 1:25-28)."

Excerpts from *Guiding Light – Feed My Soul*

p. 111 When Jesus said the two greatest commandments were about love: love of God and love of neighbor, the Jewish scholar asked Jesus another question: "And who is my neighbor?" You might recall that there was great animosity between Jews and Samaritans, so in introducing a Samaritan into the story, Jesus shows us "neighbor" could be anyone, even someone we despise.

p. 51 The conversation Jesus had about tragic events at the beginning of today's gospel was interesting. Sometimes people think when something bad happens to someone it is God's punishment. Jesus said that's not always true. He does not try to explain suffering here, but he is telling us not to be complacent, which we sometimes are. We can't think "well, if nothing bad is happening to me, it must be because I am so good." He tells us we all need to repent, i.e., to work to be better than we are.

pp. 29-30 As we celebrate Jesus' baptism, may we at the same time celebrate our own. May we rejoice in God's gift of love and life given to us, and may we live up to the high dignity with which God has blessed us.

A Priest Is a Gift from God

by Rita Ring

A Song from Jesus

by Rita Ring

REFRAIN

I come to you with great-est love, I am your lov-ing Sav-ior. I am your God, I died for you, I come to you this day.

VERSES

1. You are My pre-cious lit-tle one, I love you oh so dear-ly. Come close to Me, My lit-tle one, I loved you to My death.
2. Reach out to Me and do not fear, I want to be so close to you. You are My child, My pre-cious one, I love you ten-der-ly.

I Love You Jesus

by Rita Ring

VERSES

1. Oh Burn-ing Heart, Oh Love di - vine, how
2. I can - not say. There are not words to
3. Your ten - der Heart, Oh how it beats for

sweet You are to me. I see the host, I
say what my heart feels. I love You so, I
love of each this day. I want to give You

know You're here to love and care for me.
scarce can breathe when You come in - to me.
all my love, sur - ren - der to - tal - ly.

REFRAIN

I know Your love a lit - tle now, so

dear You are to me. Come give me life, a -

bun - dant life, I thirst to be with Thee.

The Rosary Song

by Rita Rin

REFRAIN

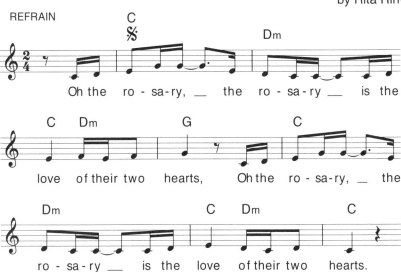

Oh the ro - sa-ry, __ the ro - sa-ry __ is the love of their two hearts, Oh the ro - sa-ry, __ the ro - sa-ry __ is the love of their two hearts.

VERSES 1-4

1. A - ve Ma - ri - a, A - ve Ma - ri - a. Oh the
2. Je - sus we love You, Ma - ry we love __ you. Oh the
3. This is her peace plan, Chil-dren must pray __ it. Oh the
4. We turn to Ma - ry, She is the Queen of Peace. Oh the

VERSE 5

No left hand

5. Oh Sa-cred Heart di - vine, Oh heart of Ma-ry pure,

A - ve Ma - ri - a, We love to pray it! Oh the

"This is My Body, This is My Blood."

Prayer Before the
Holy Sacrifice of the Mass

Let me be a holy sacrifice and unite with God in the sacrament of His greatest love.

I want to be one in Him in this act of love, where He gives Himself to me and I give myself as a sacrifice to Him. Let me be a holy sacrifice as I become one with Him in this my act of greatest love to Him.

Let me unite with Him more, that I may more deeply love Him. May I help make reparation to His adorable Heart and the heart of His Mother, Mary. With greatest love, I offer myself to You and pray that You will accept my sacrifice of greatest love. I give myself to You and unite in Your gift of Yourself to me. Come and possess my soul.

Cleanse me, strengthen me, heal me. Dear Holy Spirit act in the heart of Mary to make me more and more like Jesus.

Father, I offer this my sacrifice, myself united to Jesus in the Holy Spirit to You. Help me to love God more deeply in this act of my greatest love.

Give me the grace to grow in my knowledge, love and service of You and for this to be my greatest participation in the Mass. Give me the greatest graces to love You so deeply in this Mass, You who are so worthy of my love.

– *Mass Book*, December 27, 1995

Shepherds of Christ Associates

PRAYER MANUAL

Shepherds of Christ Publications
China, Indiana

Imprimi Potest: Rev. Bradley M. Schaeffer, S.J.
Provincial
Chicago Province, The Society of Jesus

Imprimatur: Most Rev. Carl K. Moeddel
Auxiliary Bishop
Archdiocese of Cincinnati

The Shepherds of Christ Associates Prayer Manual is published by Shepherds of Christ Publications, an arm of Shepherds of Christ Ministries, P.O. Box 627 China, Indiana 47250 USA.

Founder, Shepherds of Christ Ministries:
Father Edward J. Carter, S.J.

For more information contact:
Shepherds of Christ Associates
P.O. Box 627
China, Indiana 47250- USA
Tel. 812-273-8405
Toll Free: 1-888-211-3041
Fax 812-273-3182

First Printing, September 1994
Second Printing, November 1994
Third Printing, November 1995
Fourth Printing, March 1996

Chapter Meeting
Prayer Format

The prayer format below should be followed at chapter meetings of *Shepherds of Christ Associates*. All prayers, not just those said specifically for priests, should include the intention of praying for all the needs of priests the world over.

1. **Hymns.** Hymns may be sung at any point of the prayer part of the meeting.

2. **Holy Spirit Prayer.** Come, Holy Spirit, almighty Sanctifier, God of love, who filled the Virgin Mary with grace, who wonderfully changed the hearts of the apostles, who endowed all Your martyrs with miraculous courage, come and sanctify us. Enlighten our minds, strengthen our wills, purify our consciences, rectify our judgment, set our hearts on fire, and preserve us from the misfortunes of resisting Your inspirations. Amen.

3. **The Rosary.**

4. **Salve Regina.** "Hail Holy Queen, Mother of mercy, our life, our sweetness, and our hope. To you do we cry, poor banished children of Eve. To you do we send up our sighs, our mourning, our weeping in this vale of tears. Turn, then, most gracious advocate, your eyes of mercy toward us and after this, our exile, show unto us the blessed fruit of your womb, Jesus, O clement, O loving, O sweet Virgin Mary. Amen."

5. **The Memorare.** "Remember, O most gracious Virgin Mary, that never was it known that anyone who fled to your protection, implored your help, or sought your intercession was left unaided. Inspired by this confidence, I fly unto you, O Virgin of virgins, my

Mother. To you I come, before you I stand, sinful and sorrowful. O Mother of the Word Incarnate, despise not my petitions, but, in your mercy, hear and answer me. Amen."

6. **Seven Hail Marys in honor of the Seven Sorrows of Mary.** Mary has promised very special graces to those who do this on a daily basis. Included in the promises of Our Lady for those who practice this devotion is her pledge to give special assistance at the hour of death, including the sight of her face. The seven sorrows are:

(1) The first sorrow: the prophecy of Simeon (Hail Mary).

(2) The second sorrow: the flight into Egypt (Hail Mary).

(3) The third sorrow: the loss of the Child Jesus in the temple (Hail Mary).

(4) The fourth sorrow: Jesus and Mary meet on the way to the cross (Hail Mary).

(5) The fifth sorrow: Jesus dies on the cross (Hail Mary).

(6) The sixth sorrow: Jesus is taken down from the cross and laid in Mary's arms (Hail Mary).

(7) The seventh sorrow: the burial of Jesus (Hail Mary).

7. **Litany of the Blessed Virgin Mary.**
Lord, have mercy on us.
Christ, have mercy on us.
Lord, have mercy on us. Christ, hear us.
Christ, graciously hear us.
God, the Father of heaven, *have mercy on us.*
God, the Son, Redeemer of the world, *have mercy on us.*
God, the Holy Spirit, *have mercy on us.*

Holy Trinity, one God, *have mercy on us.*
Holy Mary, *pray for us* (repeat after each invocation).
Holy Mother of God,
Holy Virgin of virgins,
Mother of Christ,
Mother of the Church,
Mother of divine grace,
Mother most pure,
Mother most chaste,
Mother inviolate,
Mother undefiled,
Mother most amiable,
Mother most admirable,
Mother of good counsel,
Mother of our Creator,
Mother of our Savior,
Virgin most prudent,
Virgin most venerable,
Virgin most renowned,
Virgin most powerful,
Virgin most merciful,
Virgin most faithful,
Mirror of justice,
Seat of wisdom,
Cause of our joy,
Spiritual vessel,
Vessel of honor,
Singular vessel of devotion,
Mystical rose,
Tower of David,
Tower of ivory,
House of gold,
Ark of the Covenant,
Gate of heaven,

Morning star,
Health of the sick,
Refuge of sinners,
Comforter of the afflicted,
Help of Christians,
Queen of angels,
Queen of patriarchs,
Queen of prophets,
Queen of apostles,
Queen of martyrs,
Queen of confessors,
Queen of virgins,
Queen of all saints,
Queen conceived without original sin,
Queen assumed into heaven,
Queen of the most holy rosary,
Queen of families,
Queen of peace,
Lamb of God, who take away the sins of the world,
 spare us, O Lord.
Lamb of God, who take away the sins of the world,
 graciously hear us, O Lord.
Lamb of God, who take away the sins of the world,
 have mercy on us.
Pray for us, O holy Mother of God,
 *that we may be made worthy of the promises of
 Christ.*

Let us pray: Grant, we beseech You, O Lord God, that we Your servants may enjoy perpetual health of mind and body and, by the glorious intercession of the blessed Mary, ever virgin, be delivered from present sorrow, and obtain eternal joy. Through Christ our Lord. Amen.

We fly to your patronage, O holy Mother of God. Despise not our petitions in our necessities, but deliver us always from all dangers, O glorious and blessed Virgin. Amen.

8. **Prayer to St. Joseph.** St. Joseph, guardian of Jesus and chaste spouse of Mary, you passed your life in perfect fulfillment of duty. You supported the Holy Family of Nazareth with the work of your hands. Kindly protect those who trustingly turn to you. You know their aspirations, their hardships, their hopes; and they turn to you because they know you will understand and protect them. You too have known trial, labor, and weariness. But, even amid the worries of material life, your soul was filled with deep peace and sang out in true joy through intimacy with the Son of God entrusted to you, and with Mary, His tender Mother. Amen.

— (Pope John XXIII)

9. **Litany of the Sacred Heart, promises of the Sacred Heart.**
Lord, have mercy on us.
Christ, have mercy on us.
Lord, have mercy on us. Christ, hear us.
Christ, graciously hear us.
God the Father of heaven,
have mercy on us (repeat after each invocation).
God the Son, Redeemer of the world,
God the Holy Spirit,
Holy Trinity, one God,
Heart of Jesus, Son of the eternal Father,
Heart of Jesus, formed by the Holy Spirit in the womb of the Virgin Mother,
Heart of Jesus, substantially united to the Word of God,
Heart of Jesus, of infinite majesty,

Heart of Jesus, sacred temple of God,
Heart of Jesus, tabernacle of the Most High,
Heart of Jesus, house of God and gate of heaven,
Heart of Jesus, burning furnace of charity,
Heart of Jesus, abode of justice and love,
Heart of Jesus, full of goodness and love,
Heart of Jesus, abyss of all virtues,
Heart of Jesus, most worthy of all praise,
Heart of Jesus, king and center of all hearts,
Heart of Jesus, in whom are all the treasures of wisdom and knowledge,
Heart of Jesus, in whom dwells the fullness of divinity,
Heart of Jesus, in whom the Father is well pleased,
Heart of Jesus, of whose fullness we have all received,
Heart of Jesus, desire of the everlasting hills,
Heart of Jesus, patient and most merciful,
Heart of Jesus, enriching all who invoke You,
Heart of Jesus, fountain of life and holiness,
Heart of Jesus, propitiation for our sins,
Heart of Jesus, loaded down with opprobrium,
Heart of Jesus, bruised for our offenses,
Heart of Jesus, obedient even to death,
Heart of Jesus, pierced with a lance,
Heart of Jesus, source of all consolation,
Heart of Jesus, our life and reconciliation,
Heart of Jesus, victim of sin,
Heart of Jesus, salvation of those who hope in You,
Heart of Jesus, hope of those who die in You,
Heart of Jesus, delight of all the saints,
Lamb of God, Who take away the sins of the world,
    spare us, O Lord.
Lamb of God, Who take away the sins of the world,

graciously hear us, O Lord.
Lamb of God, Who take away the sins of the world,
  have mercy on us.
Jesus, meek and humble of heart,
  make our hearts like unto Yours.

Let us pray: O almighty and eternal God, look upon the Heart of Your dearly beloved Son and upon the praise and satisfaction He offers You in behalf of sinners and, being appeased, grant pardon to those who seek Your mercy, in the name of the same Jesus Christ, Your Son, Who lives and reigns with You, in the unity of the Holy Spirit, world without end. Amen.

Promises of Our Lord to those devoted to His Sacred Heart (these should be read by the prayer leader):

(1) I will give them all the graces necessary in their state of life.
(2) I will establish peace in their homes.
(3) I will comfort them in all their afflictions.
(4) I will be their refuge during life and above all in death.
(5) I will bestow a large blessing on all their undertakings.
(6) Sinners shall find in My Heart the source and the infinite ocean of mercy.
(7) Tepid souls shall grow fervent.
(8) Fervent souls shall quickly mount to high perfection.
(9) I will bless every place where a picture of My Heart shall be set up and honored.
(10) I will give to priests the gift of touching the most hardened hearts.
(11) Those who promote this devotion shall have their names written in My Heart, never to be blotted out.

(12) I promise you in the excessive mercy of My Heart that My all-powerful love will grant to all those who communicate on the first Friday in nine consecutive months the grace of final penitence; they shall not die in My disgrace nor without receiving their sacraments; My divine Heart shall be their safe refuge in this last moment.

10. **Prayer for Priests.** "Lord Jesus, Chief Shepherd of the Flock, we pray that in the great love and mercy of Your Sacred Heart You attend to all the needs of Your priest-shepherds throughout the world. We ask that You draw back to Your Heart all those priests who have seriously strayed from Your path, that You rekindle the desire for holiness in the hearts of those priests who have become lukewarm, and that You continue to give Your fervent priests the desire for the highest holiness. United with Your Heart and Mary's Heart, we ask that You take this petition to Your heavenly Father in the unity of the Holy Spirit. Amen."

11. **Prayer for all members of the Shepherds of Christ Associates.** "Dear Jesus, we ask Your special blessings on all members of Shepherds of Christ Associates. Continue to enlighten them regarding the very special privilege and responsibility you have given them as members of Your movement, Shepherds of Christ Associates. Draw them ever closer to Your Heart and to Your Mother's Heart. Allow them to more and more realize the great and special love of Your Hearts for each of them as unique individuals. Give them the grace to respond to Your love and Mary's love with an increased love of their own. As they dwell in Your Heart and Mary's Heart, abundantly care for all their needs and those of their loved ones. We make our

prayer through You to the Father, in the Holy Spirit, with Mary our Mother at our side. Amen."

12. **Prayer for the spiritual and financial success of the priestly newsletter.** "Father, we ask Your special blessings upon the priestly newsletter, Shepherds of Christ. We ask that You open the priest-readers to the graces You wish to give them through this chosen instrument of Your Son. We also ask that You provide for the financial needs of the newsletter and the Shepherds of Christ Associates. We make our prayer through Jesus, in the Holy Spirit, with Mary at our side. Amen."

13. **Prayer for all members of the human family.** "Heavenly Father, we ask Your blessings on all Your children the world over. Attend to all their needs. We ask Your special assistance for all those marginalized people, all those who are so neglected and forgotten. United with our Mother Mary, we make this petition to You through Jesus and in the Holy Spirit. Amen."

14. **Prayer to St. Michael and our Guardian Angels:** "St. Michael the Archangel, defend us in battle. Be our safeguard against the wickedness and snares of the devil. May God rebuke him, we humbly pray, and do thou, O prince of the heavenly hosts, by the power of God, cast into hell Satan and all the other evil spirits who prowl about the world seeking the ruin of souls. Amen."

"Angel of God, my guardian dear, to whom God's love commits me here, ever this day be at my side, to light and guard, to rule and guide. Amen."

15. **Pause for silent, personal prayer.** This should last at least five minutes.

16. **Act of consecration to the Sacred Heart of Jesus and the Immaculate Heart of Mary.**

"Lord Jesus, Chief Shepherd of the flock, I consecrate myself to Your most Sacred Heart. From Your pierced Heart the Church was born, the Church You have called me, as a member of Shepherds of Christ Associates, to serve in a most special way. You reveal Your Heart as a symbol of Your love in all its aspects, including Your most special love for me, whom You have chosen as Your companion in this most important work. Help me to always love You in return. Help me to give myself entirely to You. Help me always to pour out my life in love of God and neighbor! Heart of Jesus, I place my trust in You!

"Dear Blessed Virgin Mary, I consecrate myself to your maternal and Immaculate Heart, this Heart which is symbol of your life of love. You are the Mother of my Savior. You are also my Mother. You love me with a most special love as a member of Shepherds of Christ Associates, a movement created by your Son as a powerful instrument for the renewal of the Church and the world. In a return of love, I give myself entirely to your motherly love and protection. You followed Jesus perfectly. You are His first and perfect disciple. Teach me to imitate you in the putting on of Christ. Be my motherly intercessor so that, through your Immaculate Heart, I may be guided to an ever closer union with the pierced Heart of Jesus, Chief Shepherd of the flock."

17. **Daily Prayers.** All members should say the Holy Spirit prayer daily and make the act of consecration daily. They should also pray the rosary each day. They are encouraged to use the other above prayers as time allows.

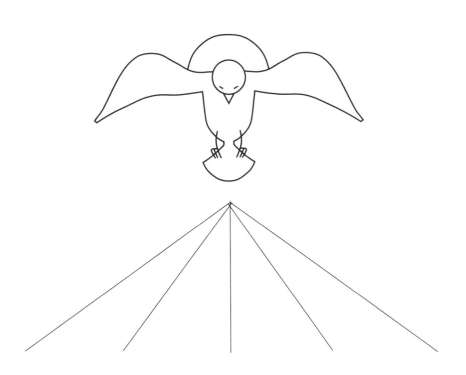

HOLY SPIRIT NOVENA

**The Holy Spirit Novnea prayers are
also available in
Spanish, French, and Portuguese.**

Shepherds of Christ Publications
China, Indiana

This book is published by Shepherds of Christ Publications, a subsidiary of Shepherds of Christ Ministries, a tax exempt religious public charitable association organized to foster devotion to the Two Hearts, the Sacred Heart of Jesus and the Immaculate Heart of Mary.

For additional copies, contact us:

Shepherds of Christ Ministries
P.O. Box 627
China, Indiana 47250 USA

(toll free number) 1-888-211-3041
(phone) 1-812-273-8405
(fax) 1-812-273-3182
http://www.SofC.org

Nihil Obstat:
Rev. Daniel J. Mahan, S.T.L.
Censor Librorum
Archdiocese of Indianapolis

Imprimatur:
Archbishop Daniel M. Buechlein, O.S.B.
Archbishop of Indianapolis
Archdiocese of Indianapolis

First Printing: March, 1999
Second Printing: April, 2000

DAILY NOVENA PRAYERS

Opening Prayer

In the name of the Father and of the Son and of the Holy Spirit. Amen.

Dear Father, we come to You in the name of Jesus, in union with Him in the Holy Sacrifice of the Mass, in the Holy Spirit. We come to You united to the Child Jesus of Good Health and the Infant of Prague. We come to You in the perfect, sinless heart of Our Mother Mary, asking her powerful intercession, uniting ourselves to her holy tears. We come to You united to all the angels and saints, and the souls in purgatory.

Prayer for Holy Spirit

We pray for an outpouring of the Holy Spirit on us, to be baptized by the Holy Spirit, that He will descend mightily on us as He did on the Apostles at Pentecost. That the Holy Spirit will transform us from fear to fearlessness and that He will give us courage to do all the Father is asking of us to help bring about the Reign of the Sacred Heart and the triumph of Mary's Immaculate Heart. We pray for the Holy Spirit to descend mightily on the Jesuits and the Poor Clares on the Shepherds of Christ leaders and members and on the whole Body of Christ and the world.

Protection by the Blood of Jesus

We pray that the Blood of Jesus will be spread on us, everyone in our families, and the Shepherds of Christ Movement, that we will be able to move steadfastly ahead and be protected from the evil one.

Healing

We pray for healing in body, mind, and soul and generational healing in ourselves, in all members in our families, and in all members of the Shepherds of Christ Movement, the Jesuit Community, the Poor Clares, the Body of Christ, and the world.

Prayer for Strength and Light

We adore You, oh Holy Spirit. Give us strength, give us light, console us. We give ourselves entirely to You. Oh Spirit of light and grace, we want to only do the will of the Father. Enlighten us that we may live always in the Father's will.

Eternal Spirit fill us with Your Divine Wisdom that we may comprehend more fully insight into Your Divine Mysteries.

Give us lights, Oh Holy Spirit that we may know God. Work within the heart, the spiritual womb of the Virgin Mary, to form us more and more into the image of Jesus.

Prayer to Be One with God, Father, Son and Holy Spirit

We long for You, Oh Spirit of Light, we long to know God, we want to be one with Him, our Divine God. We want to be one with the Father, know Him as a Person most intimately. We want to know the beloved One, the Sacred Heart of Jesus, and live and dwell in Him at all times, every moment of our lives. We want to be one with You, Oh Spirit of Light, that You move in us in our every breath.

Prayer to Be One in Jesus

Let us experience life in the Sacred Heart of Jesus, so we can say as Saint Paul, "I have been crucified with Christ and yet I am alive; yet it is no longer I, but Christ living in me...." Let us live, united to the Mass, all through the day being one in Him. Let us be able to love and know in this elevated state of oneness with our God. We long for Thee, oh beauteous God, we love You, we love You, we love You. We praise You, worship You, honor You, adore You, and thank You, our beloved God, Father, Son, and Holy Spirit.

Prayer to Dwell in the Hearts of Jesus and Mary

We seek to be one in God, to live and dwell in the Hearts of Jesus and Mary, our little heaven on earth, to experience life in the all perfect, pure, sinless heart of our Mother. We want the Holy Spirit to move in us and to be united to Jesus as the Bridegroom of our souls and be a most perfect sacrifice offered to the Father at every moment as we unite in the Holy Sacrifice of the Mass around the world to help in the salvation of souls.

Prayer for the Holy Spirit and His Gifts

Come Holy Spirit, come, come into our hearts, inflame all people with the fire of Your love.

Leader: Send forth Your Spirit and all will be reborn.

All: And You will renew the face of the earth.

We pray for the seven gifts of the Holy Spirit, we ask for perfection in our souls to make us holy, holy souls likened to God.

Dear Holy Spirit, we give ourselves to You soul and body. We ask You to give us the Spirit of Wisdom, Understanding, Counsel, Fortitude, Knowledge, Piety, and Fear of the Lord.

Prayer for the Word Alive in Our Hearts

We know, dear Holy Spirit, the Word in His human nature was brought forth within the womb of the woman. We pray that His word will be brought forth in our hearts as He lives and dwells in us. We want the incarnation to go on in our lives. Dear Holy Spirit, work in us.

Little Prayers to the Holy Spirit

Dear Holy Spirit, help us not to be ignorant or indifferent or weak, help us to be strong with the love of God.

Dear Holy Spirit, please pray for our needs for us.

Dear Holy Spirit, help us to respect God and to avoid sin. Help us to live in the Father's will.

Dear Holy Spirit, help us to keep Your commandments and to respect authority. Help us to love all things as You will us to love them. Help us to want to pray and always serve God with the greatest love. Help us to know the truth. Help us to have the gift of faith, hope, and love. Help us to know what is right and what is wrong.

A Prayer for Intimacy with the Lamb, the Bridegroom of the Soul

Oh Lamb of God, Who take away the sins of the world, come and act on my soul most intimately. I surrender myself, as I ask for the grace to let go, to just be as I exist in You and You act most intimately on my soul. You are the Initiator. I am the soul waiting Your favors as You act in me. I love You. I adore You. I worship You. Come and possess my soul with Your Divine Grace, as I experience You most intimately.

FIRST WEEK
MEDITATIONS NINE DAYS

1. **Romans 8:14-17**
All who are guided by the Spirit of God are sons of God; for what you received was not the spirit of slavery to bring you back into fear; you received the Spirit of adoption, enabling us to cry out, 'Abba, Father!' The Spirit himself joins with our spirit to bear witness that we are children of God. And if we are children, then we are heirs, heirs of God and joint-heirs with Christ, provided that we share his suffering, so as to share his glory.

2. **Romans 8:5-9**
Those who are living by their natural inclinations have their minds on the things human nature desires; those who live in the Spirit have their minds on spiritual things. And human nature has nothing to look forward to but death, while the Spirit looks forward to life and peace, because the outlook of disordered human nature is opposed to God, since it does not submit to God's Law, and indeed it cannot, and those who live by their natural inclinations can never be pleasing to God. You, however, live not by your natural inclinations, but by the Spirit, since the Spirit of God has made a home in you. Indeed, anyone who does not have the Spirit of Christ does not belong to him.

3. **1 John 4:12-16**
No one has ever seen God, but as long as we love one another God remains in us and his love comes to its perfection in us. This is the proof that we remain in him and he in us, that he has given us a share in his Spirit. We ourselves have seen and testify that the Father sent his Son as Saviour of the world. Anyone who acknowledges that Jesus is the Son of God, God remains in him and he in God. We have recognised for

ourselves, and put our faith in, the love God has for us. God is love, and whoever remains in love remains in God and God in him.

4. 1 John 4:17-21

Love comes to its perfection in us when we can face the Day of Judgement fearlessly, because even in this world we have become as he is. In love there is no room for fear, but perfect love drives out fear, because fear implies punishment and no one who is afraid has come to perfection in love. Let us love, then, because he first loved us. Anyone who says 'I love God' and hates his brother, is a liar, since whoever does not love the brother whom he can see cannot love God whom he has not seen. Indeed this is the commandment we have received from him, that whoever loves God, must also love his brother.

5. 1 John 4:7-11

My dear friends, let us love one another, since love is from God and everyone who loves is a child of God and knows God. Whoever fails to love does not know God, because God is love. This is the revelation of God's love for us, that God sent his only Son into the world that we might have life through him. Love consists in this: it is not we who loved God, but God loved us and sent his Son to expiate our sins. My dear friends, if God loved us so much, we too should love one another.

6. Acts of the Apostles 1:1-5

In my earlier work, Theophilus, I dealt with everything Jesus had done and taught from the beginning until the day he gave his instructions to the apostles he had chosen through the Holy Spirit, and was taken up to heaven. He had shown himself alive to them after his Passion by many demonstrations: for forty days he had continued to appear to them and tell them about the kingdom of God. While at table with them, he had told them not to leave Jerusalem, but to wait there for what the Father had promised. 'It is', he had said, 'what you have heard me speak about: John baptised with water but, not many days from now, you are going to be baptised with the Holy Spirit.'

7. Acts of the Apostles 1:6-9

Now having met together, they asked him, 'Lord, has the time come for you to restore the kingdom to Israel?' He replied, 'It is not for you to know times or dates that the Father has decided by his own authority, but you will receive the power of the Holy Spirit which will come on you, and then you will be my witnesses not only in Jerusalem but throughout Judaea and Samaria, and indeed to earth's remotest end.'

As he said this he was lifted up while they looked on, and a cloud took him from their sight.

8. Acts of the Apostles 1:12-14

So from the Mount of Olives, as it is called, they went back to Jerusalem, a short distance away, no more than a Sabbath walk; and when they reached the city they went to the upper room where they were staying; there were Peter and John, James and Andrew, Philip and Thomas, Bartholomew and Matthew, James son of Alphaeus and Simon the Zealot, and Jude son of James. With one heart all these joined constantly in prayer, together with some women, including Mary the mother of Jesus, and with his brothers.

9. Acts of the Apostles 2:1-4

When Pentecost day came round, they had all met together, when suddenly there came from heaven a sound as of a violent wind which filled the entire house in which they were sitting; and there appeared to them tongues as of fire; these separated and came to rest on the head of each of them. They were all filled with the Holy Spirit and began to speak different languages as the Spirit gave them power to express themselves.

SECOND WEEK
MEDITATIONS NINE DAYS

1. John 14:21-31

Whoever holds to my commandments and keeps them is the one who loves me; and whoever loves me will be loved by my Father, and I shall love him and reveal myself to him.'

Judas—not Judas Iscariot—said to him, 'Lord, what has happened, that you intend to show yourself to us and not to the world?' Jesus replied:

'Anyone who loves me will keep my word, and my Father will love him, and we shall come to him and make a home in him. Anyone who does not love me does not keep my words. And the word that you hear is not my own: it is the word of the Father who sent me. I have said these things to you while still with you; but the Paraclete, the Holy Spirit, whom the Father will send in my name, will teach you everything and remind you of all I have said to you. Peace I bequeath to you, my own peace I give you, a peace which the world cannot give, this is my gift to you. Do not let your hearts be troubled or afraid. You heard me say: I am going away and shall return. If you loved me you would be glad that I am going to the Father, for the Father is greater than I. I have told you this now, before it happens, so that when it does happen you may believe.

'I shall not talk to you much longer, because the prince of this world is on his way. He has no power over me, but the world must recognise that I love the Father and that I act just as the Father commanded. Come now, let us go.

2. John 17:11-26

I am no longer in the world, but they are in the world, and I am coming to you. Holy Father, keep those you have given me true to your name, so that they may be one like us. While I was with them, I kept those you had given me true to your name. I have watched over them and not one is lost except one who was destined to be lost, and this was to fulfil the scriptures. But now I am coming to you and I say these things in the world to share my joy with them to the full. I passed your word on to them, and the world hated them, because they belong to the world no more than I belong to the world. I am not asking you to remove them from the world, but to protect them from the Evil One. They do not belong to the world any more than I belong to the world. Consecrate them in the truth; your word is truth. As you sent me into the world, I have sent them into the world, and for their sake I consecrate myself so that they too may be consecrated in truth. I pray not only for these but also for those who through their teaching will come to believe in me. May they all be one, just as, Father, you are in me and I am in you, so that they also may be in us, so that the world may believe it was you who sent me. I have given them the glory you gave to me, that they may be one as we are one. With me in them and you in me, may they be so perfected in unity that the world will recognise that it was you who sent me and that you have loved them as you have loved me.

Father, I want those you have given me to be with me where I am, so that they may always see my glory which you have given me because you loved me before the foundation of the world. Father, Upright One, the world has not known you, but I have known you, and these have known that you have sent me. I have made your name known to them and will continue to make it known, so that the love with which you loved me may be in them, and so that I may be in them.

3. 1 Corinthians 15:20-28

In fact, however, Christ has been raised from the dead, as the first-fruits of all who have fallen asleep. As it was by one man that death came, so through one man has come the resurrection of the dead. Just as all die in Adam, so in Christ all will be brought to life; but all of them in their proper order: Christ the first-fruits, and next, at his coming, those who belong to him. After that will come the end, when he will hand over the kingdom to God the Father, having abolished every principality, every ruling force and power. For he is to be king until he has made his enemies his footstool, and the last of the enemies to be done away with is death, for he has put all things under his feet. But when it is said everything is subjected, this obviously cannot include the One who subjected everything to him. When everything has been subjected to him, then the Son himself will be subjected to the One who has subjected everything to him, so that God may be all in all.

4. Revelation 3:1-3,12,16-19

'Write to the angel of the church in Sardis and say, "Here is the message of the one who holds the seven spirits of God and the seven stars: I know about your behaviour: how you are reputed to be alive and yet are dead. Wake up; put some resolve into what little vigour you have left: it is dying fast. So far I have failed to notice anything in your behaviour that my God could possibly call perfect; remember how you first heard the message. Hold on to that. Repent! If you do not wake up, I shall come to you like a thief, and you will have no idea at what hour I shall come upon you.

Anyone who proves victorious I will make into a pillar in the sanctuary of my God, and it will stay there for ever; I will inscribe on it the name of my God and the name of the city of my God, the new Jerusalem which is coming down from my God in heaven, and my own new name as well.

'...but since you are neither hot nor cold, but only lukewarm, I will spit you out of my mouth. You say to yourself: I am rich, I have made a fortune and have everything I want, never realising that you are wretchedly and pitiably poor, and blind and naked too. I warn you, buy from me the gold that has been tested in the fire to make you truly rich, and white robes to clothe you and hide your shameful nakedness, and ointment to put on your eyes to enable you to see. I reprove and train those whom I love: so repent in real earnest.'

5. Revelation 5:9-14

They sang a new hymn: You are worthy to take the scroll and to break its seals, because you were sacrificed, and with your blood you bought people for God of every race, language, people and nation and made them a line of kings and priests for God, to rule the world.

In my vision, I heard the sound of an immense number of angels gathered round the throne and the living creatures and the elders; there were ten thousand times ten thousand of them and thousands upon thousands, loudly chanting:

Worthy is the Lamb that was sacrificed to receive power, riches, wisdom, strength, honour, glory and blessing. Then I heard all the living things in creation—everything that lives in heaven, and on earth, and under the earth, and in the sea, crying:

To the One seated on the throne and to the Lamb, be all praise, honour, glory and power, for ever and ever.

And the four living creatures said, 'Amen'; and the elders prostrated themselves to worship.

6. Revelation 7:14-17

I answered him, 'You can tell me, sir.' Then he said, 'These are the people who have been through the great trial; they have washed their robes white again in the blood of the Lamb. That is why they are standing in front of God's throne and serving him day and night in his sanctuary; and the One who sits on the throne will spread his tent over them. They will never hunger or thirst again; sun and scorching wind will never plague them, because the Lamb who is at the heart of the throne will be their shepherd and will guide them to springs of living water; and God will wipe away all tears from their eyes.'

7. Revelation 12:1-8

Now a great sign appeared in heaven: a woman, robed with the sun, standing on the moon, and on her head a crown of twelve stars. She was pregnant, and in labour, crying aloud in the pangs of childbirth. Then a second sign appeared in the sky: there was a huge red dragon with seven heads and ten horns, and each of the seven heads crowned with a coronet. Its tail swept a third of the stars from the sky and hurled them to the ground, and the dragon stopped in front of the woman as she was at the point of giving birth, so that it could eat the child as soon as it was born. The woman was delivered of a boy, the son who was to rule all the nations with an iron sceptre, and the child was taken straight up to God and to his throne, while the woman escaped into the desert, where God had prepared a place for her to be looked after for twelve hundred and sixty days.

And now war broke out in heaven, when Michael with his angels attacked the dragon. The dragon fought back with his angels, but they were defeated and driven out of heaven.

8. Revelation 14:1-7

Next in my vision I saw Mount Zion, and standing on it the Lamb who had with him a hundred and forty-four thousand people, all with his name and his Father's name written on their foreheads. I heard a sound coming out of heaven like the sound of the ocean or the roar of thunder; it was like the sound of harpists playing their harps. There before the throne they were singing a new hymn in the presence of the four living creatures and the elders, a hymn that could be learnt only by the hundred and forty-four thousand who had been redeemed from the world. These are the sons who have kept their virginity and not been defiled with women; they follow the Lamb wherever he goes; they, out of all people, have been redeemed to be the first-fruits for God and for the Lamb. No lie was found in their mouths and no fault can be found in them.

Then I saw another angel, flying high overhead, sent to announce the gospel of eternity to all who live on the earth, every nation, race, language and tribe. He was calling, 'Fear God and glorify him, because the time has come for him to sit in judgement; worship the maker of heaven and earth and sea and the springs of water.'

Revelation 19: 7-8

let us be glad and joyful and give glory to God, because this is the time for the marriage of the Lamb. His bride is ready, and she has been able to dress herself in dazzling white linen, because her linen is made of the good deeds of the saints.'

9. Revelation 21:1-10

Then I saw a new heaven and a new earth; the first heaven and the first earth had disappeared now, and there was no longer any sea. I saw the holy city, the new Jerusalem, coming down out of heaven from God, prepared as a bride dressed for her husband. Then I heard a loud voice call from the throne, 'Look, here God lives among human beings. He will make his home among them; they will be his people, and he will be their God, God-with-them. He will wipe away all tears from their eyes; there will be no more death, and no more mourning or sadness or pain. The world of the past has gone.'

Then the One sitting on the throne spoke. 'Look, I am making the whole of creation new. Write this, "What I am saying is trustworthy and will come true." ' Then he said to me, 'It has already happened. I am the Alpha and the Omega, the Beginning and the End. I will give water from the well of life free to anybody who is thirsty; anyone who proves victorious will inherit these things; and I will be his God and he will be my son. But the legacy for cowards, for those who break their word, or worship obscenities, for murderers and the sexually immoral, and for sorcerers, worshippers of false gods or any other sort of liars, is the second death in the burning lake of sulphur.'

One of the seven angels that had the seven bowls full of the seven final plagues came to speak to me and said, 'Come here and I will show you the bride that the Lamb has married.' In the spirit, he carried me to the top of a very high mountain, and showed me Jerusalem, the holy city, coming down out of heaven from God.

Revelation 22:20

The one who attests these things says: I am indeed coming soon.

Amen; come, Lord Jesus.

Scriptural quotations are taken from
The New Jerusalem Bible, Doubleday & Co.
Imprimatur granted by Cardinal Hume.

Prayer for Union with Jesus

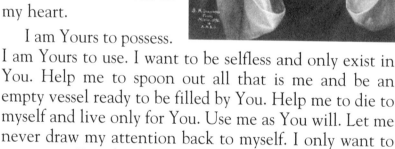

Come to me, Lord, and possess my soul. Come into my heart and permeate my soul. Help me to sit in silence with You and let You work in my heart.

I am Yours to possess. I am Yours to use. I want to be selfless and only exist in You. Help me to spoon out all that is me and be an empty vessel ready to be filled by You. Help me to die to myself and live only for You. Use me as You will. Let me never draw my attention back to myself. I only want to operate as You do, dwelling within me.

I am Yours, Lord. I want to have my life in You. I want to do the will of the Father. Give me the strength to put aside the world and let You operate my very being. Help me to act as You desire. Strengthen me against the distractions of the devil to take me from Your work.

When I worry, I have taken my focus off of You and placed it on myself. Help me not to give in to the promptings of others to change what in my heart You are making very clear to me. I worship You, I adore You and I love You. Come and dwell in me now.

150 Year Celebration of St Boniface as a Parish and Father Joe's 50th Celebration of Ordination

IN REMEMBRANCE
OF MY
FIFTIETH ANNIVERSARY
OF PRIESTLY ORDINATION

Rev. JOSEPH A. ROBINSON
1964   MAY   2014

Let us Pray for one another

Baptism

Eucharist

Confirmation

Confirmation

Marriage

Rita Robinson Ring and Fr. Joseph Robinson

Other great books published by Shepherds of Christ Publications

(To order call or write us at address in front of book)

Shepherds of Christ Prayer Manual
The Shepherds of Christ has prayer chapters all over the world praying for the priests, the Church and the world. These prayers that Father Carter compiled in the summer of 1994 began this worldwide network of prayer. Currently the prayers are in eight languages with the Church's *Imprimatur*. We have prayed daily for the priests, the Church, and the world since 1994. Associates are called to join prayer Chapters and help us circulate the newsletter centered on spreading devotion to the Sacred Heart and Immaculate Heart and helping to renew the Church through greater holiness. Please form a Prayer Chapter & order a Prayer Manual. Item P1 - $0.50

Spirituality Handbook Fr. Edward Carter, S.J. did 3 synopsis of the spiritual life. *The Spirituality Handbook, the Priestly Newsletter 2000 Issue 3* and the *Tell My People* book. The way of spiritual life proposed to the members of Shepherds of Christ Associates is centered in consecration to the Hearts of Jesus and Mary. All aspects of the spiritual life discussed below should be viewed as means to help members develop their lives in consecration to Christ, the Sacred Heart, and to Mary, the Immaculate Heart. Item P2 - $3

Fr. Edward J. Carter S.J.

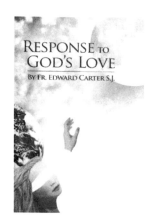

Response to God's Love by Fr. Edward J. Carter, S.J. In this book Fr. Carter speaks of God as the ultimate mystery. We can meditate on the interior life of the Trinity. Fr. Carter tells us about our uniqueness in the Father's Plan for us, how the individual Christian, the Church and the world are in the state of becoming. *Imprimatur*. Item BN4 -$10

Shepherds of Christ - Selected Writings on Spirituality for all People as Published in Shepherds of Christ Newsletter for Priests. Contains 12 issues of the newsletter from July/August 1994 to May/June 1996. Item BN1 - $15

Shepherds of Christ - Volume 2 by Fr. Edward J. Carter, S.J. Contains issues 13-29 of the Priestly newsletter (September / October 1996 - Issue 5, 1999) Item BN2 - $15

Fr. Edward J. Carter S.J.

Shepherds of Christ - Volume 3 by Fr. Edward J. Carter, S.J. Contains Priestly Newsletter Issues 1 through 4 of 2000 including Fr. Carter's tremendous *Overview of the Spiritual Life*
Item BN3 - $10

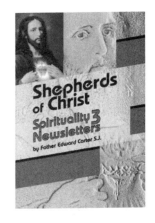

Rita Ring

Mass Book, by Rita Ring. Many of the entries in the Priestly Newsletter Volume II from a spiritual journal came from this book. These entries are to help people to be more deeply united to God in the Mass. This book is available in English and Spanish with the Church's *Imprimatur*.
Item B8 - $12

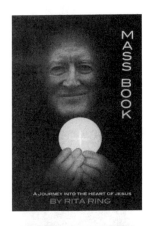

Parents and Children's Rosary Book, by Rita Ring. Short Meditations for both parents and children to be used when praying the rosary. These medi-tations will help all to know the lives of Jesus and Mary alive in their Hearts. Available in both English and Spanish with the Church's *Imprimatur*.
Item B7 - $10

Fr. Joe Robinson
(Rita Ring's Brother)

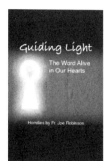

Guiding Light - The Word Alive in Our Hearts. - **Cycle A** (partial) — Homilies by the Reverend Joe Robinson given at St. Boniface Church in Cincinnati, Ohio. It is a tremendous honor Fr. Joe has allowed us to share these great gifts with you – for greater holiness and knowing more and more about God. Item C1 - $5

Guiding Light - Focusing on the Word - Cycle B — At times we may feel that our path to Christ is a bit "out of focus". Like the disciples in the Book of Mark, this ordinary life clouds our vision of Christ's Divinity. We may doubt the practicality or possibility of applying His teachings and example to our modern life. Cycle B's homilies are a "guiding light" to help us realize Jesus' Messianic greatness and His promise of better things to come. Item C2 - $15

Feed My Soul - Cycle C — In a world rapidly advancing and encouraging personal gain, we are faced with modern problems. There is a challenge to find time in our busy schedules for Sunday Mass or a family meal. We are able to research, shop, bank and even work without hearing one human voice. It is no wonder that we may often feel disconnected and famished at our week's end. In Fr. Joe's third book of homilies from Cycle C, we are reminded of the charity that Christ intended us to show each other. .... We are rewarded with the Father's kingdom and love when we are not worthy. We are not left alone or hungry. C3 - $15

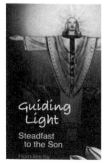

Steadfast to the Son - Cycle A — The sunflower is a great example of how we should be steadfastly guided by light. What a powerful thought that this exceptional plant is not stuck in one pose day in and day out, yet adaptable and magnetized to the sun. We feel the same about our Son. Our heads turns to face Christ as each day presents its challenges to find light. We join together like plants in a field and soak up the Son through the pulpit. We are a warm circle of strength using the wind of our breath to carry our priests' words, Christ's words, to new rich soil. Item C4 - $15

Guiding Light - Reflect on the Word - Cycle B — The Word leaves an impression on our souls. In my thoughts and reflections are born a more tangible understanding of these eternal concepts presented in the Gospels and the readings. Anyone can read a sentence, but not anyone can absorb it's true meaning. Truth, in this day and age, is almost a matter of opinion or individual entitlement. We believe that Christ's truth is our Roman Catholic Church. We, as priests, champion it's teachings; we are ambassadors for the Pope and Christ to those faces looking at us. We are the light by which our congregation reads to reflect upon real truth and we do it hand in hand. Item C5 - $15

Guiding Light - Centered In Christ, Cycle C — In the gospel of St. Luke, Christ turns toward Jerusalem, making the choice of love through sacrifice. In the silence of our own hearts, we find a worthy call to action. What personal path will you chose as you center in Jesus Christ? Fr. Joseph Robinson has dedicated his life to serving Christ and the Church from the Cincinnati Archdiocese in Ohio for over 40 years. He inspires his parishioners with the homilies found in these pages. ... May they be a guiding light for you as they have been for so many others. Item C6 -$10

Guiding Light - Inspired To Be Genuine, Cycle A

We look over the pulpit, like a father over Sunday breakfast and we want to connect. We want our parishioners to know the fulfillment, wisdom and desire that inspired our vows. We want them to find Christ and each other in Christ. Like a father, we want their attention, love and respect.

Privately, their minds may be else-where: in the next meeting, compiling a grocery list, worrying about a child, or angry with their spouse. We all leave a proverbial tornado of obligatory noise at the church doors to enjoy a single hour of unhurried glory. ... Father Joe Robinson inspires this appreciation into focus with humor, interesting facts and fresh perspectives. His homilies are easily followed, yet "meaty". May we all succeed to enliven a tangible God in the heart's forefront of those who hear us. Item C7 - $10

Featured Selections

Response in Christ by Fr. Carter

The book, *Response in Christ,* comes at a very opportune time. In a thoughtful blend of the traditional and the modern, Fr. Carter gives to the modern Christian a message that will sustain him.

The most promising aspect of the book is Fr. Carter's gift about the Spiritual life. The Christian life essentially consists in God's loving self-communication to us with our response to Him in love. God gives us a sharing in His life in baptism. This life is nourished by the Eucharist. Father Carter offers reflections on how to deepen one's relationship with God: Father, Son and Holy Spirit. Item BN5 -$10

By God Through Me by Fr. Joe Robinson

It can be challenging to remain alive to the magnitude of the role that I perform as a priest, a servant of God, a shepherd to the world, a sacramental sign of Christ... I wake up, eat, brush my teeth, get dressed and then transform bread into Flesh and wine into Blood.

Each Sunday, I look into all those faces. One is given new life by God through me in Baptism. Another is forgiven by God through me in Reconciliation. They are all loved by God through me. A troubled mother-to-be guided by God through me. My words can impact life or death decisions! This reality can sometimes seem surreal, but the glory remains, whether I am in the moment or not. May we all be blessed with mindfulness and a thankful nature. May these pages, in full or in part, provide a springboard to captivate your flock! May God bless you as a guiding light to all. -$10

Shepherds of Christ Ministries

(You may copy this page to order.)

<u>Send Order To:</u>
Shepherds of Christ Ministries
P.O. Box 627
China, Indiana 47250 USA

Order Form

	Qty	Total $
P1. Prayer Manuals ($0.50)	____	_____
P2. Spirituality Handbook ($3)	____	_____
BN1. Shepherds of Christ - Volume 1 ($15)	____	_____
BN2. Shepherds of Christ - Volume 2 ($15)	____	_____
BN3. Shepherds of Christ - Volume 3 ($10)	____	_____
BN4. Response to God's Love ($10)	____	_____
BN5. Response in Christ ($10)	____	_____
B7. Parents and Children's Rosary Book($10)	____	_____
B8. Mass Book ($12)	____	_____
C1. The Word Alive in Our Hearts ($5)	____	_____
C2. Focusing on the Word - Cycle B ($15)	____	_____
C3. Feed My Soul - Cycle C ($15)	____	_____
C4. Steadfast to the Son - Cycle A ($15)	____	_____
C5. Reflect on the Word - Cycle B ($15)	____	_____
C6. Centered in Christ - Cycle C ($10)	____	_____
C7. Inspired To Be Genuine - Cycle A ($10)	____	_____
C8. By God Through Me - Cycle B ($10)	____	_____
Totals:	____	_____

Name: _____

Address: _____

City: _____ State: _____ Zip: _____

For More Information Call Toll free USA: 1-888-211-3041
or on the Internet: www.sofc.org

We pray for you from our Church in China,
24 hours a day before the exposed Eucharist.
We pray eight-day retreats for you every month.